P9-BYR-928

Contents

The Questions to Ask Before You Jump Into Bed

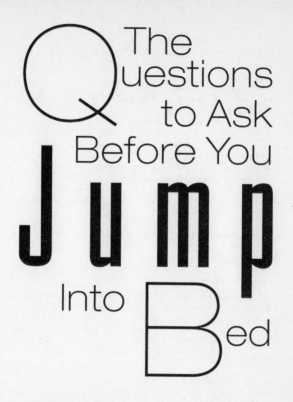

The Questions to Ask Before You Jump Into Bed

What to bring up before you get down

LAURIE SEALE

A PERIGEE BOOK

THE BERKLEY PUBLISHING GROUP
Published by the Penguin Group
Penguin Group (USA) Inc.
375 Hudson Street, New York, New York 10014, USA
Penguin Group (Canada), 90 Eglinton Avenue East, Suite 700, Toronto, Ontario, M4P 2Y3, Canada
(a division of Pearson Penguin Canada Inc.)
Penguin Books Ltd., 80 Strand, London WC2R 0RL, England
Penguin Group Ireland, 25 St. Stephen's Green, Dublin 2, Ireland (a division of Penguin Books Ltd.)
Penguin Group (Australia), 250 Camberwell Road, Camberwell, Victoria 3124, Australia
(a division of Pearson Australia Group Pty. Ltd.)
Penguin Books India Pvt. Ltd., 11 Community Centre, Panchsheel Park, New Delhi—110 017, India
Penguin Group (NZ), Cnr. Airborne and Rosedale Roads, Albany, Auckland 1310, New Zealand
 (a division of Pearson New Zealand Ltd.)
Penguin Books (South Africa) (Pty.) Ltd., 24 Sturdee Avenue, Rosebank, Johannesburg 2196,
South Africa

Penguin Books Ltd., Registered Offices: 80 Strand, London WC2R 0RL, England

Copyright © 2005 by Laurie Seale
Text design by Ellen Cipriano
Cover art and design by Ben Gibson

PRINTING HISTORY
Perigee trade paperback edition / November 2005

PERIGEE is a registered trademark of Penguin Group (USA) Inc.
The "P" design is a trademark belonging to Penguin Group (USA) Inc.

Library of Congress has cataloged the original Perigee trade publication as follows

Seale, Laurie.
    The questions to ask before you jump into bed / Laurie Seale.
        p.   cm.
    ISBN 0-399-53205-6
    1. Mate selection.   2. Dating (Social customs)   3. Sex.   I. Title.
    HQ801..S4419 2005
    646. 7'7   dc22

                                                                    2005047636

PRINTED IN THE UNITED STATES OF AMERICA

10 9 8 7 6 5 4 3 2 1

Dedication

For Sharon, for asking what my philosophy was. For Lisa, more sister and more creative soul mate than friend. For Susan, for suggesting every day for one full year that I join her in yoga class. For Heather Feather, my darling dearest baby sister, who is so much like me and so much *not* like me; for all your hurt, sorrow, suffering you've endured and all your loving endless belief in me, your staunch support; to all those who said it couldn't be done, you said, "She will do it." For Elizabeth and Brenda, who while supporting me also found and married their soul mates in the four years it has taken me to see this project to completion. Natasha—this project could not have been done without your dedication, insight, brilliance, and faith in me. And Christel for sharing my vision and making my job so easy. You are the women who give my life humor, value, and substance—who help me remain connected to myself and to life.

Steve—while we were not meant to be, may you and your new wife be blessed by a God who loves, recognizes, and accepts us all. Mark, may the world receive your brilliance and may the stage of life welcome your compositions with open arms. And Joseph—never has there been a man whom I have felt so intellectually addicted to. To Pavel, who taught me what unconditional love felt like. To G., wait for me, you say—wait for me, I say. Trey, for finding Natasha—my beam of light in the darkest of nights, and the best agent and friend an author could hope to have.

To my dearest aunt Kay, for all the hours of laughter, bike riding, and all the casual conversations that sealed my confidence as a woman.

For Mom and Dad. I was so lucky to have you both. And all you did for me and continue to do for me.

And Andy Pandy. For a brother who wouldn't quit until he found his sister. So much so you'd drive all night long looking for me while I sat in Waco, Texas. Forever I will remember the night when I opened the door and saw you standing there smiling, laughing that I'd forgotten to tell you which hotel I was at.

And all the others who've taught me the art of loving, the art of complementary compatibility. May you all find the love you seek . . . the love that will bring you and your partner a lifetime of euphoric joy and happiness.

Namaste,
Laurie

Foreword

American singles have no trouble getting physically naked, but what about baring their emotions?

We came of age at a time when premarital sex was expected and endorsed. At a time when society, our peers, and even our parents have come to expect us to be sexually involved if we're dating. But isolated sexual involvement without the context for someone's values will not create a foundation for a lifetime partnership. And with one in two marriages ending in divorce—it is imperative we examine our behavior and acknowledge our own culpability. Incompatible values do not emerge during the "high" of dating, the "lust" of new sex, or the fun of the "wedding party."

Incompatibilities emerge when the day-to-day of getting along becomes a priority and you realize you do not have the necessary skills, values, or commitment to the partnership. You can choose to be one of two, or you can choose a different way to approach partnering. It's your choice, your life, and your emotional health.

Nakedness, sex, and even foreplay can distract us, which leads us further away from emotional intimacy. In fact, we have trivialized the act of sharing our bodies so much so that anyone can have sex with "no strings attached"—and this is perceived as normal. We give these encounters euphemistic names such as "booty calls," or "friends with benefits," to blunt their meaning. Former president Bill Clinton has infamously stated that oral sex is not really sex at all, and as a society, we've accepted this—oral sex is *not* sex, intimate, nor sharing, it's just an exchange. This preference for physical intimacy before emotional intimacy has only come at a high cost, including:

+ Our inability to restrain ourselves when we find someone we are interested in pursuing on a more serious level. We would like to behave differently, but we fall victim to old behavior patterns.
+ The inability to stop the cycle of using others for our own immediate pleasure and short-term satisfaction. Invariably when a relationship does not evolve toward the expectations we have, at

least one person gets hurt. We have lost the ability to tell which partners are genuinely interested in us for a relationship of emotional, intellectual, and spiritual value, and forgotten how to avoid those who are pursuing sexual gratification.

✦ The inability to be emotionally open and vulnerable. We have become guarded and withdrawn because of painful experiences in our past. By withholding from our partners our deepest fears, our biggest insecurities, our grandest dreams; what in essence composes the reality of who we really are—we lose what makes us real and relatable in a relationship.

✦ Even when we do open up, we've developed an inability to accept others for who *they* are once we see their emotionally naked selves.

Self-actualization, increased self-esteem, and greater acts of selflessness make opportunistic behavior—such as sex for your own selfish gratification—less alluring—in fact it becomes distasteful. We regulate our own behavior, restricting ourselves not because someone else has said "don't do this," but because we feel better about ourselves when we treat others with kindness and respect. At the end of the day, we don't get any awards for doing the right thing, taking the high road, or behaving honorably.

However, we do get something much more valuable: the

sense of who we rightfully are, what we believe in, and the realization that we are willing to behave honorably even when tested with temptation. This honor code is not one we righteously wear as a badge of dutiful behavior; rather it is a karmic energy that draws another to us—one who respects values, and behaves in the same manner towards us. We stop doing what we can get away with, and start behaving with kindness and respect; inviting a deeper form of loving. Just because someone is willing to share him or herself physically does not give us the justification to take from them indiscriminately. We are individually responsible for our actions, and the sexual permissiveness of another does not give us a right to take, especially if we know or suspect we might not be there for them the next day, the next month, the next year. Abstaining from sex, foreplay, and other sexual intimacies ensures both people are treated respectfully and kindly. Abstaining until both partners give absolute commitment, and demonstrate acceptance of each other, sets the stage for an authentic and deeper love.

True soulful intimacy comes when two people are willing to be emotionally naked. You see how their words and behavior create a mosaic of consistency, one which comprises their values, ethics, and humanitarian spirit. How do you know when you can trust what you hear and what you see them do? You see this consistency for days, weeks, months on end, until eventually, your vision is true and clear when your partner stands physically naked before you.

True soul mates can be naked emotionally and spiritually; compatible, not just based on one value, but many. They are partners who do not quit on one another or the partnership they are creating together, who are committed to accepting one another unconditionally. Only when this moment of true connection and commitment is reached should one elect to enhance a relationship by becoming physically involved.

But this is not the message taught to us, fed to us daily by the media. It is, however, the path to finding love without end, love without limits: your Divine love.

What I propose in the following pages is, I believe, an alternative to what the media portrays. Rather than the approach we've adopted since the sexual revolution, this is a healthy, constructive, and productive, philosophy for finding a lifetime partner. I believe this philosophy not only makes the best use of one's time, but also enables us to be emotionally open to new experiences. One can experience the building of trust, and love, while deconstructing the cynicism, which surrounds dead end relationships, as well as breaking down the emotional barriers that prevent true intimacy. This philosophy can reunite the mind, body, and soul, such that sexual experiences are both physically rewarding as well as emotionally gratifying.

Why have we lost our patience? Why are we not willing to discover the core of another person's value system? Why are we confused about what a soul mate really is? Why has divorce become the social solution to incompatibility? What does compatibility actually look and feel like? Within these pages, you will find answers to these questions and more. Read on . . .

Introduction

An Author's Confessions: Asking for Forgiveness from Myself

I wrote this book in 2001 thinking I had some insight I'd like to share with a friend. I rewrote it in 2002 with what felt like two lifetimes' worth of humility to humble and temper any life lessons I might share with a larger audience. And I rewrote it for a third time in 2004 after having included yoga in my life, identifying my own spirituality, engaging in a few more relationship experiences, and finally, completing a lifelong learning cycle. So I've had some time to not only digest my philosophy but to live with it, practice it, incorporate it into my own life, and fully feel the challenge of self-discipline I am asking of you. I know because I have asked it of myself and know how challenging it can be, and more so, feel. But I have also had the time to assimilate the philosophy and know resolutely, without a doubt, it is the healthiest approach to love.

A Yogic Approach to Love

The philosophy I propose is contrary to the sexual media messages we receive every day, and it is also a way to interact with others that lets you emotionally engage, present your most authentic self, be grounded, centered, loving, and available to what life brings you, knowing when to engage further and when to extract yourself. And from all of these actions you receive freedom. Freedom to move and to live and to feel without only feeling hurt, angry, dejected, or sad.

The philosophy I present is a mechanism for authentic engaging and loving without hurting in a modern twenty-first-century world where it would seem there are no rules for love and everyone is out for themselves. This is a journey toward self-actualization.

I have made my most unhealthy partnership choices when I wasn't in an emotionally healthy place myself. When we partner with people, we are getting something out of it. Even if our most spiritual or emotional needs are not being met, some need(s) are being fulfilled or else we wouldn't be engaging in that relationship.

In the past, I partnered with people out of a lack of self-awareness of what is most complementary and fulfilling to me. From each experience a piece of the puzzle was filled in. The philosophy presented are the puzzle pieces I believe and know in my soul to be the pieces you need to lead you to a greater depth of self-awareness, and to your partner: your soul mate, the person you are most compatible with to spend the rest of your life with in a loving, fulfilling relationship.

There is one piece of the puzzle that completes the picture, and that is self-discipline. It's not something I can give you; it's something you must exercise. I can guide you toward self-awareness, but I cannot give you self-discipline to apply what you learn in these pages to your next encounter. I can get you closer to your partner, to the brink, in fact, but ultimately it will require self-discipline. I will show you how to recognize from the people you meet whether they are compatible with you or not, but it will take self-discipline from you to walk away when you identify those who are not most compatible—despite how sexy they are, despite some single great connection you have. I will show you how many qualities and values you need in common for a fulfilling partnership and how to recognize them.

I believe a healthy relationship is built on a pyramid, a foundation, if you will, that looks like this (working from the bottom to top):

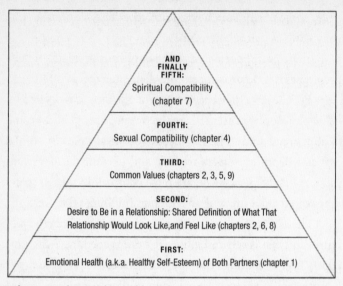

The Pyramid Toward a Healthy Relationship and Fulfilling Partnership

At each level, there are questions that will help you identify if the qualities for that level are present. I believe you can
have a loving, fulfilling partnership with the first four tiers.
In other words, it's not absolutely necessary for a fulfilling
relationship to have a common spirituality. But in my research of levels of happiness (Maslow), levels of fulfillment
(Maslow), levels of self-esteem (Brandon), individuals reach
the highest state of personal fulfillment when they are serving something beyond themselves, when they are serving humanity in some capacity. The path toward serving humanity,
toward alleviating the suffering of others, will place you on a

spiritual path. When you share this with a partner it will elevate your relationship to new zeniths. The two of you will be bound by a phenomenal expression of love, compassion, kindness, and selflessness toward each other and the world.

How to Know if You'll Be Compatible *Out* of Bed

From the pyramid, you can see that each level requires a level of self-actualization and self-awareness. This is where you have the opportunity to manifest your self-discipline, for it takes self-discipline to not give in to headlong temptation. It takes self-discipline to not bypass what will become the foundation of your partnership and simply jump into bed before discovering whether you would be compatible *out* of bed. It takes self-discipline to spend time with yourself now making sure you know the real you. It takes self-discipline to become the most brilliant, beautiful, healthy you.

I'm ready to share what I have learned from a lifetime of experiences and studying people. Walk this journey with me and you will never again wonder "Is he right for me?" "Can she create a fulfilling relationship with me?" "I wonder who is right for me?"

Included you'll find the questions to ask before you jump into bed, but before you can begin, I have one question for you:

Are you ready?

If so, let's begin. Prepare to have some fun along the way because what's on the other side is the magnificent, self-aware you.

one

All About Me

How well do you know yourself?

Know Yourself: You're the Foundation of Your Own Relationship

Until you know yourself, who you are and what you value, your entire definition of self is at the disposal of someone else to manipulate, shape, and approve. Think of Julia Roberts's character in *Runaway Bride*. Her character was beautiful; thus, she always found herself the object of men's attention. However, she had never taken the time to figure out who she was or what she liked, so she was constantly adjusting her sense of self to complement a different partner. It wasn't until Richard Gere's character demonstrated to Julia's character how her preference for fried, scrambled, or poached eggs was at the mercy of each fiancé's selection.

But Julia, who had been so busy planning weddings and spending time with men who found her attractive, hadn't spent the time developing her own self-awareness and self-identity. Egg preference may be a trivial example, but it is one that illustrates how relevant it is to know your values and how your preferences and priorities make you unique and the value of partnering with someone who can appreciate, value, and accept your individuality—and complement it as well.

Thus, if you don't know who you are or what you like, you are surrendering that power of identity to someone else to endorse or approve of you. Sometimes we are attracted to someone because we admire something we wished we possessed—maybe their commitment to personal growth, their fastidiousness, their aptitude with money, or their self-discipline for working out.

However, while you may admire these qualities in another, until you yourself become those, actually embody those traits, you cannot expect a partner who already possesses them to find you a compatible match until you yourself do so.

Dating Isn't Personal

If you do not have a clear understanding of who you are and what you value, dating feels like one big risk of personal rejection. But once you understand who you are and what you value, you make much better decisions in terms of who you are attracted to, and you choose only those who are compatible with your values because you know choosing your opposite or someone who doesn't share your values is a waste of time: they will not value you, will not see you as a treasure, a gift. Likewise, once you possess self-confidence about who you are, you stop interpreting their lack of interest as rejection and understand that they desire some other (not better or worse) qualities in a partner.

Socrates said, "Know yourself." And I concur. Because when you know yourself, you are on the road to self-acceptance, and self-acceptance leads to loving yourself—the first step in the journey toward finding another to love. You may think you can, but you cannot *possibly* begin to love another before you know who you are, and really love the person you are, foibles and all.

You can summarize all your dating experiences in the following categories:

Self-Awareness
+ People you've chosen because you don't know yourself well enough to realize how incompatible they are with your values.
+ People you've chosen because you have not yet reached the place where you love and fully accept yourself; thus, desiring another like you.

Self-Discipline
+ People you've partnered with, ignoring that they can't give you what you desire, but you choose them in a moment of weakness, loneliness, or sadness, and it's just a matter of time before you admit they aren't enough and you find the strength, courage, and resolve to leave them.

In my twenties, I had a series of boyfriends who fell into the first two categories, but it wasn't until my mid-thirties, when I experienced the humility that accompanies becoming involved with someone in the third category. Age and experience increased self-awareness, but didn't make me immune from occasional loneliness and the ability to rationalize a "less-than" choice as okay for awhile. Self-awareness is extremely empowering and freeing—when practiced with a lot of self-discipline.

The challenge is understanding yourself, becoming your

own values, forgiving yourself for what you believe might have been wrong decisions, and finally arriving at love for yourself. And once you arrive at this juncture, you then possess the self-esteem and discipline to avoid those who cannot give you what you desire. You also arrive at a place where your cup runneth over with fulfillment in life such that you don't find yourself making inappropriate partner choices because you are lonely, frustrated, resentful, or feel empty. When you reach the place of solid self-love, you have manifested into your life *all that you value* and this gives you so much joy and fulfillment that you aren't lonely or sad. You have made peace with the past, you live in the moment, and don't worry about the future. You become the most beautiful, loving version of you.

When you truly accept yourself, really accept yourself *As Is,* and love who you are, you stop filtering messages through a siphon of insecurity, of not being enough, or not having enough. And instead you just act as you are. Authentic. Content.

As a former columnist for a large online dating site, I regularly received emails of people asking me what they should do in dating situations. I was struck by one in particular when a woman emailed me and asked what she should wear on a first date. She had asked a friend if leather pants were appropriate. The friend had advised her that leather would send the wrong message. I was more curious about the message she was sending if her date had known how riddled with doubt she was about what to wear and what his reaction to her would be. My answer was simple: please yourself and not someone else; wear whatever makes you feel comfortable, sexy, confident. And let the date interpret whatever message he wants. You could beleaguer the decision only to settle on khakis and he might draw the conclusion that you had a Katharine Hepburn boy complex. I told her to stop worrying so much about how someone perceives her and focus more on how she perceives herself. If someone is interested in you, they'll take the time to ask and understand you, your context, your world—whether it's leather pants on the first date or your libertarian political views. You can spend your whole life, and dating life, guessing and trying to predict and adapt to how others will see you. Moreover, physical appearance is so superficial. Someone might have on exactly the clothes you perceive as cool, beautiful, hip, and sexy, and fail to possess inside the genuine qualities of trust, honesty, and integrity.

Present your most genuine honest self. And this is what I mean by healthy self-esteem, and good emotional health. When you are emotionally healthy, and have solid self-esteem, you present your most genuine self. *As Is* means you have the courage from a strong sense of self to reveal your most genuine self at all times because you like who you are and what you believe in; moreover you accept who you are. In front of all people. That's emotional health and solid self-esteem.

When I jokingly ask people, "How do you come?" I am waiting for the retort of, "As is." Most people love the concept of telling the world to take them for who they are, but few really appreciate or understand the ramifications of acting in accordance with that philosophy. If you hate sushi, don't say you like it. If you don't condone abortion, don't say you do. If you want five children, express that. If you love your hair long and someone likes it short, don't cut it to please him. To be loved for who you are, you have to present who you really are. If you let someone guess who you are, you run a tremendous risk that they will guess incorrectly and project values onto you that you do not possess, and then they will be disappointed and so will you. Express who you are, in all your glory, foibles, and eccentricities.

I have a vulnerability for European men and I was once spending time with a German orthodontist while he was vacationing in the States. My friends asked how we were getting along and they were curious if a language barrier existed between us. I confessed that he had told me his ex-girlfriend of nine years had beautiful long hair and a different physique than mine. When I asked him how she was different than me, he said I had a butt like a twelve-year-old boy and my stomach looked like I was three months' pregnant. Then I laughed and told my girlfriends, "You tell me if it's a language barrier or cultural difference in how they seduce women." I was bemused by his comments. At the time I was teaching teach five spinning classes a week, 3 abs classes, and he knew I was a former runway model turned ad executive. I pride myself on expressing my creativity in all things physical, and at the time that included a very distinct, urban short haircut. I'm quite confident in how I look and who I am. That's why I was so bemused. After he told me this, I looked at him and said, "You can take it or leave it." He looked at me, startled, and said, "Did you interpret that I wasn't attracted to you or didn't find your body or appearance appealing by what I said?" Cultural differences, I suppose. The point is that it didn't bother me. In fact, it became a joke between us for the duration of his vacation and for weeks afterward when he returned to see me again, and again.

If you are reading this, then you, too, obviously value self-discovery and awareness—and only with awareness can we begin to love ourselves. People who protect and value their self-esteem have an avowed commitment to continued self-awareness and self-actualization. When you can say, "Yes, I love who I am," it means you believe in yourself. Your internal messaging every day is positive; you are not berating yourself with negative messages of "I can't," or "It's not possible," or "I'm not worthy," or other negatives.

That fact that you can say, right now, today, "I accept who I am, including the mistakes I've made. And I not only like myself, but I love myself, As Is," is a reflection of positive self-esteem and this is where you must begin on the journey toward loving another.

What Does Self-esteem Have to Do with My Decision about Who I Partner with or When?

It has everything to do with it. Self-esteem is at the core of happiness. And it is the foundation for a healthy relationship. Healthy, committed, enduring relationships require two people—not one—who are emotionally healthy. And both people must have a very firm definition of self, and this heightened self-awareness of who they are and what they believe in enables them to have healthy self-esteem. Self-esteem is directly related to our ability to trust others. And it is directly linked to our ability to let another demonstrate love toward us. How receptive we are to gestures of kindness and love (do you accept them gracefully or are you skeptical of them?) is a reflection of our self-image.

When you know what you value and who you are, you make life decisions to accomplish more positive things. These conscious decisions of identifying what you need, moving toward it, and accomplishing it positively validate your self-esteem. It's a cycle that I call "challenge/complete." Most people think that the worst thing that could happen to them would be to not have something they desire. Not so. It is far worse to not know what you are moving toward or from. You've seen people like this. They are just going through the motions of life, lacking direction, lacking exuberance, passion, joy. They are more or less coasting without a driving excitement toward anything.

Connecting to passion and joy and sheer exuberance for something you love to do is what makes you feel your life has value, that you are connecting to something larger than yourself and something that matters. When these feelings are absent and there's just the rote routine of the day, a person drowns in a general malaise because they have stopped challenging themselves. We see people like this all the time: people who stopped doing their homework on what makes them happy, who let fear dominate their life so much so they stop pursuing what gives them joy. This is not someone you want as a partner. You want someone who has clear and distinct purpose, ambition, and is driving forward with happiness not because they are running away *from* something, but *toward* something. You can distinguish between the two by observing if people are joyful about what they do and if they are achieving balance in their life.

A lack of focus or definition means you are operating without a sense of security. Friends often asked me how I found the courage to quit advertising and become a full-time author and artist. My answer is that I was willing to gamble the security of a corporate job against the confidence in myself to move toward new goals, such that even in moments when my world would appear to be an unpredictable maelstrom, I had the reassurance that at the core was a very centered, focused person driving forward with passion and joy. I replaced the security of a twice-a-month paycheck with the security that I was pursuing something I loved, relished, and was tremendously challenging, and that I felt served a larger purpose toward the good of humanity, not just the good of a corporation. No one said running forward toward a dream was easy. There have been days, nights when I thought, "Uh oh, what next?" but all the time, I was filled with joy for what I was doing and infused with pride that I could make it work and humility of hope. Accomplishment breeds accomplishment. And the accomplishments just grow in proportion to your confidence in yourself.

I have often heard that you will draw into your world your mirror image. Metaphorically, people are referring to the idea that you will attract someone who is in the exact same mental space you are. I beg to differ. Confident people who have a strong sense of self radiate happiness because they are pursuing that which is important to them. And happiness draws all kinds of attention. Someone who is attracted to your sense of self may or may not be in the same healthy space as you. But the more self-aware you become, the easier it is to recognize where others are and decipher whether they are attracted to you because they, too, are in a healthy space in life, or because they wish they were and know you are and want to see how you got there.

Understanding and reaching a place of genuine self-esteem has many advantages. For one, you make much healthier decisions about who to include in your life. Two, it becomes much easier to see who is genuinely in a place to give you what you desire, avoid those who can't, and decipher mixed signals from others.

You also learn how to pace your emotional involvement while still becoming emotionally engaged. If you've ever been attracted to someone and just given yourself to them hoping they would catch you, only to feel the thud of your butt landing on the floor when they didn't, then you understand the concept of pacing your emotional involvement to match the rate of their disclosure.

Three, you feel better about life in general. You are genuinely happy and content with yourself and life. And you are okay whether you are alone or with a companion. By developing yourself and concentrating on the things you need to accomplish to feel good about your identity, you nurture yourself with positive validation every day.

Fourth, happiness breeds happiness. When you have developed the skill set to create happiness in your world you also have developed the skill set to protect your state of contentment, both in the present and in the future. Moreover, not only is it a good place to be in for yourself, but you become much more attractive to others. Positive energy begets positive, healthy energy.

There's just one catch: You can't fake genuine happiness and contentment with yourself. You have to find it by identifying what you value and what you desire in your life and having an action plan to get you there. My friends have often remarked that despite what happens in my life, I seem to adapt. The ability to adjust to life's unpredictability is a sign of healthy self-esteem. And it doesn't mean that I don't experience sadness, hurt, or disappointment; I do. But I also don't wallow in negative feelings. I spend time figuring out how the situation developed, how I am going to remedy it, making a plan for a different course and then moving forward. You, too, have the power, creativity, imagination, and strength to create the world you desire.

What are signs of healthy self-esteem?

Famed psychologist Dr. Abraham Maslow and Dr. Kennon Sheldon of the University of Missouri both believed that low self-esteem was the root of many psychological issues. I concur. I believe we create dysfunctional relationships as a result of the feelings we have about ourselves. If we felt better about ourselves we would of course manifest better, happier, in essence more fulfilling, rewarding, and enriching relationship experiences in our lives.

The number one predictor of a relationship's success is the psychological health of each partner. In other words, the emotional health or self-esteem of each partner will determine the quality of the relationship.

Therefore, if you desire the most fulfilling relationship possible, you yourself must reach the highest level of development possible and find someone else who complements that path.

This necessity for both people to have a high level of self-esteem rules out the vast majority of relationships you see around you today by the virtue that one or both individuals is not in a healthy place. Once you learn to recognize what healthy self-esteem looks like and feels like you can begin to work on your own, and recognize it in others. You will learn to avoid even entering relationships with those who are simply not in a place to give.

Where do relationships start?

It all begins with you. With your relationship with yourself. Until you are truly happy with who you are and what you are doing with your life, you will not draw into your life the most fulfilling and rewarding relationship.

Nathaniel Branden, Ph.D., in *The Art of Living Consciously* says at the core of developing self-esteem is an inherent need for the conscious mind to learn to trust itself. Consciousness is volitional in that we can choose whether we elect to think or not, how conscious to be, how present to our actions. Thus, whether we learn how to function in our lives is a conscious choice. We are not victims unless we choose to be. And every thought is moving us either toward greater consciousness or away. Toward clarity of mind, toward truth, or moving in the opposite direction.

This chapter will be one of the most challenging because it involves asking yourself the tough questions and analyzing what has happened in your past. Here's the good news: you can decide today to simply accept yourself and when you do, you are giving yourself permission to review past behavior without labeling it as bad or wrong, but simply review and understand it, and thus, move forward.

We cannot ask another what we are unwilling to ask and answer ourselves. Of all the judgments we pass in life, none is more important than the judgment we pass on ourselves.

How do you reach a place where you aren't afraid to ask and answer the questions of yourself or another? Decide today to accept yourself exactly as you are. It's that simple. You just decide to accept yourself. Then create a list of things you need in your life to feel fulfilled. See how many of those are present. Whatever is missing, write down a plan for how to get there. Lose weight. Pay off debt. Get a new job. Resolve to end a relationship you know isn't rewarding.

From here you have a road map for bringing into your life everything you value. Begin today on just one of those things and see how good it makes you feel. Tomorrow, do the same. And see how it makes you feel. Before you know it, you'll feel in control of your life and feel empowered toward your own happiness. This is self-esteem in action.

How well do you know yourself?

Knowing your true self is the key to your happiness and your ability to create a rewarding relationship. If you do not know what makes you happy or fulfilled, two things occur:

+ You do not reach your potential and your general malaise about life permeates your existence, affecting your sense of value, happiness, and life.
+ You select people based on one, two, or maybe three of the qualities you seek and romanticize these to justify your decisions. As an example, think of the couple who have nothing in common other than their sexual desire for one another, yet neither can exit the relationship.

If you do not spend the time now deciding what makes you happy and creating a course of life that fulfills you in every aspect, you will always find yourself in dating situations that I call Negative Selection: you date people you kind of like, but lack qualities that would make you really happy. The way you become in tune to your need for this particular missing quality is by dating people who *don't* have it. This is not healthy or productive.

One of the first questions in my book that I have often posed to people is:

* Do you want to date yourself? Why? Or why not?

Men always think it's a trick question. But it's not. It's another way of asking, Do you like yourself?

Some people believe that the idea of being so pleased with yourself that you want to date yourself is vain. On the contrary, I believe it is a reflection of someone who is emotionally healthy and has healthy self-esteem, someone who is self-aware and self-fulfilled and desires another who shares the same values. The idea of dating your opposite (explored more fully in chapter 4) is a romantic myth for people who have not evolved to become what they value, so they date their opposite. This internal strife is really against themselves and their own lack of resolve about who they are.

Popular philosophy says that money, fame, or luxury are the main factors that drive people. But you might be surprised to learn that Dr. Abraham Maslow disagreed. By studying motivation in subjects ranging from monkeys to human geniuses, he developed his widely quoted *Hierarchy of Needs* with self-actualization at the very top of needs. To show the real source of today's young man's positive experience, Dr. Kennon Sheldon of the University of Missouri refined

Maslow's theories, and then proved them with an experiment. He asked university students to recall the most satisfying events in their lives. The students derived most satisfaction from self-esteem, relatedness (relationships with other people), autonomy (being in control), and competence (being productive). They derived minimum satisfaction from popularity, influence, money, or luxury. Stoic philosophy is likely to help you capitalize on those sources of internal harmony identified by Sheldon. Lack of internal peace (commonly thought of as self-actualization) might be one of the most important factors that prevents people from reaching the highest state of self-awareness and thus self-fulfillment. [http:www.supermemo.com/articles/genius.htm]

What is self-esteem? What does it look like?

In *The Art of Living Consciously*, Nathaniel Branden writes, "Self-esteem is an experience. It is a particular way of experiencing the self. It is a good deal more than a mere feeling. It involves emotional, evaluative, and cognitive components. It also entails certain action dispositions: to move toward life rather than away from it; to move toward consciousness rather than away from it; to treat facts with respect rather than denial; to operate self-responsibly rather than the opposite."

Self-acceptance. Self-awareness. Self-love. It is difficult to accept others or have compassion for others until you completely accept and love yourself. Thus, self-love—not arrogance—is part of the path of self-discovery. From self-love you gain the self-discipline to avoid those on a different spiritual path, and only give yourself to someone who can appreciate you wholly.

Authentic self

Self-esteem gives you the confidence to present your most authentic self. What is authentic self? Presenting who you really are, not an artificial, contrived version based on what you think someone expects you to be or might want you to be, but instead presenting your true self, what you really like and dislike. When you are able to honestly present your authentic self, you are confident in how others respond to you. And when dating experiences don't produce the desired results, you don't view it as personal rejection but rather an awareness that you are seeking a different kind of personality for the greatest compatibility.

When you are your most authentic self you are a conduit for spiritual love to move through you, and you serve as a conduit to the most powerful energy forces in the world: love, compassion, peace, serenity, and grace. The way you feel when you are your most authentic, loving self is content with who you are and the world. As such you draw people to you as you draw people to a light in the night: you become an inspiration for others to move to the shore. As a conduit you then have to have the self-discipline to wait while your light shines brilliantly until someone sees it. Nothing to prove. Nothing to gain. No manipulation, just honest, real, authentic love and compassion and a sense of who they are. Not naked and vulnerable but naked and available to receive and to give.

How to recognize self-esteem in others, how to develop it, and what it means to the relationship when people have it or don't

How can you develop a healthy, loving relationship if you do not feel positive about yourself? If you are not able to honestly address choices and experiences you have made in the past? And what if your partner, too, is unwilling to discuss his past?

The answer: you cannot develop a relationship until both of you are in a healthy emotional place to do so. Otherwise, everything you do, every experience, every disagreement is run through this filter that's skewed about the world, communication, responsibility, compassion, love, and how you behave toward someone you love or desire to build intimacy with.

Building Self-esteem

As defined by Nathaniel Branden in *The Six Pillars of Self-Esteem*, self-esteem is "confidence in our ability to think, to cope with the basic challenges of life, and in our right to be successful and happy." Self-esteem also involves how we value ourselves and how we perceive our value to others. Self-esteem gives us the strength to take charge of our lives and to grow and learn from our experiences. Self-esteem is how we value and perceive ourselves and how valuable we think we are to others. Self-esteem affects how we trust others, our relationships, our work, and all aspects of our lives. Positive self-esteem gives us the strength and flexibility to take charge of our lives and grow from our mistakes without feeling rejected.

Become the person you value and respect

Jumping into bed with someone before you know if they are emotionally healthy or *if* they share your values is self-destructive behavior. And while casually jumping into bed with someone is a practice accepted by society, this behavior does not contribute toward building compatible, enduring relationships.

The decline of American values has permeated the bedroom and our relationships until the decline has become so insidious we take it as the norm. But it's not. Behavior that continues to lead to unhappiness is just self-destructive. Until you are willing to slow down and to honestly ask yourself where you are and where another is and suspend emotional, physical, and intellectual attachment until you know what this person has to give or where they are in life, is to walk a path of self-destruction.

You are obviously interested in a different approach or you wouldn't be reading this now. The new approach is asking questions of yourself and another. Begin here and see what you learn about who you are and what brings you the greatest happiness in life.

If you asked just one question, what would you ask?

Do you love yourself?

Before you know how someone is going to respond to your acts of giving, there's a question of paramount importance: How does he treat himself? And more important, does he love himself? If he can't say, Yes, I love myself, then it doesn't matter what else follows. It doesn't matter that he'll buy you the moon. Sell you the stars. Or promise you a trip around the world. Someone can promise you the moon and never be able to deliver it, because he is unable to function in a loving, nurturing relationship until he loves himself and accepts himself. You can find a way to work around the fact that one person is staying up late at night and the other is going to bed early by respecting the other's work schedule and allocating together time that works for both partners' schedules. But there's no working around someone who doesn't love himself. And the reason is simple: all of his actions, gestures, and emotions are coming from a center that's skewed, incomplete, unhappy, and certainly not mentally at peace. No matter what external happiness or wealth he seems to have, a relationship with this type of person will not be very rewarding. When someone can say, "Yes, I love myself," it means he is operating from a center within himself called self-acceptance, self-love. And having accepted himself, he is in a healthier position to accept another's point of view. Another's way of doing things. And just another person in his life.

The link between self-esteem and the questions

The more you understand who you are and what you find gratifying, the more you are able to chart a course to pursue those things in your life. As you pursue those activities and experiences in life, you nurture your self-esteem. In this way, you are building a repertoire of experiences that support your values.

People who are living their values know their values and

have experiences to support them. In this way you can use the questions to help you understand who you are, but also whether someone you're interested in actually has the experiences to support what he believes. Is he living his stated values, or is he just talking about them?

And if you are ready to begin the process of self-understanding now, here are questions to consider.

Questions of Self

Do you love yourself?

Do you accept yourself? What don't you accept? What would you like to change? Mentally? Physically? Emotionally?

What do you love about yourself?

How do you define who you are?
    A. Career
    B. Interests
    C. Family
    D. Other (specify)

What skills do you naturally possess that you wish you could be paid for?

Do you have a dream that seems so outlandishly impossible that the mere possibility of it being fulfilled fills you with both euphoria and fear? What is it? Are you moving toward it?

Do you listen as well as you converse?

When are you at your best?

What does your best look like?

When are you at your worst?

What does your worst look like?

Have you ever met someone who you thought had an intoxicating personality? What aspect of their personality drew you in?

What's your greatest joy/passion?

Which movie is your favorite of all time?

Which pet did you, or do you, love most?

What's your favorite holiday? Why?

Do you believe the adage, You are what you drive? If yes, what are you?

What's your dream car? Where would you drive it?

What's something you do that you secretly believe is indulgent and lavish, but you do it anyway because you enjoy it?

As a man, what do you do that you're proud of that puts you in touch with your feminine side? Or as a woman, your masculine side?

What comedian do you find most funny?

Are you a planner or a procrastinator?

What's your favorite color?

What's your dream vacation?

If you could invent a holiday, what would it be?

What's your idea of a great holiday?

Do you believe in magic?

Do you enjoy whimsy?

Do you believe in charms?

What do you do to relax?

Do you take the same route to work every day?

Do you drive like you talk?

Have you ever missed an important meeting because you overslept? What did you do?

Have you ever had late fees for: mortgage/rent? Car payment? Bills/credit card? Library books? Video rental? Taxes? City tickets? Other?

Whom have you most misunderstood after a first impression?

What's your favorite time of the year?

How do you manage your time?

Are you ever late? What counts as late?

Are you obsessively on time? Chronically early?

Do deadlines make you anxious?

Have you ever made a date wait? How long?

You have an appointment to keep where your timely presence is imperative to the outcome. Which one of the following scenarios best describes you?

A. You take the route you know, even though you'll be ten minutes late.
B. You take the shortcut directions someone gave you, hoping to arrive on time.

Do you expect someone to call if they are not going to be on time? Do you extend that same courtesy? Do you follow the ten-minute rule?

What's the most flattering adjective someone could use to describe you?

What's the most offensive adjective someone could use to describe you?

What's the best compliment you've ever received?

How do you accept compliments?

Which problems are you likely to confront head-on?

Which problems are you likely to procrastinate about?

What were three major turning points in your life?

What do you think the next turning point will be?

Do you run away from problems or toward them?

When have you felt lucky in life?

What do you say when someone asks, "What do you do?"

What do you say when someone asks, "How come you're not married?"

If you're divorced, what do you say when someone asks, "Why did you get a divorce?"

How do you introduce yourself?

If I had a crystal ball and said, "I know where you are going to be in six months or a year," would you want to know? Why or why not?

Which of the following would you least like to deal with:
  A. You're by yourself, and your car breaks down, miles from a service station

B. You return from Las Vegas having lost a month's worth of income
C. You have to put an employee on probation for unsatisfactory performance
D. You have to tell your lover that the way he is touching you (or kissing you) isn't quite cutting it
E. You have to return a garment without the receipt, weeks after you bought it
F. You have just enough money for three out of four of your bills, which means you have to call to request an extension
G. You have just lost your job and have to find another
H. Your partner tells you he has betrayed you
I. You must return to your college weight
J. You must navigate a foreign country all by yourself
K. You must face a tax audit
L. You must confront your best friend and admit a wrongdoing
M. You must confront your partner and tell him something he won't want to hear

What of your possessions, living area, or emotional past is off-limits to discussion? Does that ever change?

Your partner is trying to get your attention. What can you absolutely, not for any reason, be interrupted from to respond to them?

What's been the greatest tragedy(ies) in your life?

What are you most ashamed of in life?

What's the difference between guilt and remorse? When have you felt either?

What mistakes have you made in life?

How many times have you made the same mistake?

Are you mature? In what way? Immature? How?

Have you departed from what you learned as a child? Why?

How has your morality changed as you have matured?

Where are you in life? Does this surprise you?

What's the one material thing you possess that you would never surrender?

Which of your possessions should you probably surrender?

What has been life's sweetest surprise?

What story have you told no one?

What has been the hardest thing for you to change about yourself?

What's the first question you ask people when you meet them? Why?

What have you done that most typifies your personality?

What makes you laugh and cry out loud when you're alone?

What motivates you to get out of bed?

What motivates you to crawl into bed?

What are you most afraid of losing control of in your life?

Where are you going?

Where have you been?

Do you look backwards while moving forward?

Have you ever gone around something instead of through it?

How do you respond in a crisis?

What makes you lose your temper?

What makes you melt for another?

What embarrasses you?

How do you cover when you're embarrassed?

Do you remember names after being introduced the first time?

How do you shake hands?

How do you define your personal space?

When do you let someone into your personal space?

What has someone done for you that you've treasured all your life?

Have you ever had a muse?

What is it about art that makes you say you could have done that—be it a film, book, painting, or fashion? Have you ever actually gone off and done your own version of that?

Have you ever been homesick? When?

Have you ever done anything compulsive? What? If not, why not?

Have you ever done anything lavish? What?

Do you consider yourself right-brained or left-brained?

Have you ever been the object of someone else's humor? How'd it make you feel?

A stranger passes and you admire them. Do you usually verbalize compliments or only think them?

What are you most self-conscious about regarding your own appearance?

What's the most beautiful sound you've ever heard?

What makes you giggle?

What sound makes you uncomfortable?

When was the last time you cried? Were you alone?

When is there a quiet time in your mind?

Did you ever want to change your name?

What's your nickname? Who gave it to you?

What are you smart about?

Do you think you're photogenic?

When someone is verbally attacking you, how do you respond?

Have you ever looked a gift horse in the mouth? What was the gift?

Do you remember your dreams?

Do you dream in color or black and white?

What gives you nightmares?

What keeps you up at night?

If you could erase a memory that haunts you, which one(s) would it be?

What bores you?

How are you childlike?

Do you like to play?

Do you believe in rules?

Do you follow the rules? Has it harmed you or another?

What games do you play with yourself?

Do you let others play games with you?

How many Get Out of Jail Free passes does someone get before you evict them from Park Place?

Do you monopolize conversations?

What are you apathetic about?

Have you ever failed a test in school? What have you failed at in life?

Do you believe grades are a good indication of intelligence?

Are you book smart or street smart?

When have you applied street smarts to get yourself out of a predicament?

Has anyone ever described you as savvy?

Has anyone ever described you as humorous or funny?

Have you ever been labeled haughty?

Have you ever been called naughty?

What's the difference between confidence and arrogance? Which one more closely applies to you?

Is curiosity something only for children?

What throws you into a frenzy?

Are you patient?

Who is best at testing the limits of your patience?

When things are not going the way you would hope, what do you tell yourself?

Would you put your family through derision to become a political appointee or to be elected to public office?

What's the greatest misperception people have of you?

What's your physical age?

What's your mental age?

What's your spiritual age?

What's your actual age?

If they are all the same, why is that so? And if different, why?

How have your priorities changed over the past year? The past five years?

What are your priorities and goals for the upcoming year?

What are the three things you fear the most?

How do you apply creativity to living?

How do you apply creativity to playing?

How do you apply creativity to problem-solving?

How did you move past a time of self-doubt?

If I said, Life's a banquet, what would you say?

Are you passive-aggressive?

What do you do well that seems to come effortlessly?

What do you do well that you have to make a conscious effort to do?

When someone tells you there's room for improvement in your life, what are they most likely referring to?

When someone makes a suggestion for change in your life how do you respond?

Who can most easily put you on the defensive when it comes to a suggestion of change about your life? And on the contrary, who can suggest a change in your life and you are receptive to it? What's the difference between the people or suggestions they give you—i.e., what about one person puts you at ease and another on the defensive?

Do you subscribe to the "Theory of Shoulds" in life? As in, I *should* be married by this age; I *should* take this job or leave that one; I *should* have children?

What do you feel pressured to do?

If you could pick only one or the other, would you choose to increase your looks or your wealth by 20 percent?

What causes you to worry?

What limits you from reaching your goals?

What is normal?

Do you think you're normal?

What was your last adventure?

When was your life most out of control? The most in control?

Which do you prefer: structure or freedom?

What have you been most ignorant about in your life?

What city best describes your personality? Why?

What's the worst quality you inherited from your parents?

Which four people have been the most influential in your development?

What makes you feel like a child again?

What three things are always coming out of your mouth?

What's more rewarding: the journey toward a goal or attaining it?

What are you loyal to? Who are you loyal to?

What have you procrastinated doing in the last month? Year? Your life?

What's your favorite thing about yourself?

If you became a millionaire overnight how would your life change?

Does the idea of your fifteen minutes of fame thrill or terrify you? Why?

Does speaking in front of a crowd excite or terrify you? Why?

What are you curious about?

What makes you nervous?

What does your body do that gives your nervousness away?
How do you cover it?

What's intoxicating about you?

What's the difference between listening and hearing?

Do you believe you can "own" your feelings? What does
that mean to you?

What have you done in your life that's significant
to you?

What have you done that's significant to
your family?

What have you done that's significant to
your friends?

When in your life was your confidence most severely
shaken? How did you recover?

When you walk by a mirror, do you look at yourself?

When you feel relaxed, what has put you there?

What else gives you that feeling of relaxation?

What physical gestures do you consider to be signs of affection with a stranger? Lover? Sibling? Girlfriend? Boyfriend? Mom? Dad?

What kind of first impression do you think you make?

Do you lend credence to the value of first impressions?

Who is most likely to underestimate your ability? Your potential?

When are you at your absolute worst temperament? When you are:

    A. angry

    B. around animals (which ones?)

    C. around children

    D. around your parents

    E. driving your car

    F. cold

    G. feeling on the defensive

    H. furious

    I. feeling ten pounds overweight

J. hungry

K. irritated

L. overly hot

M. suffering from PMS

N. riding in a car

O. tired

P. worried about money

Q. sick

R. other (specify)

What time is it? In your day? In your life?

Was there an occasion when you hurried through something and later really wished you had taken more time?

Where do you want to be at this time next year?

What's been the biggest waste of your time?

If you lived in a neighborhood where your neighbors kept their Christmas lights up all year or didn't keep their lawns as manicured as yours, would it annoy you?

What risks do you take? Physically? Intellectually? Financially? Emotionally?

Do you have a plan for retiring?

Where do you want to retire?

At what age do you want to retire?

What makes a house feel like a home?

Have you donated anything to charity? What was it motivated by?
    A. Tax refund
    B. Cleaning effort
    C. Another person's need

Do you misplace things?

Do you believe abortion should be legal?

Do you believe in the death penalty?

Should gay couples have the right to health care?

Should gay couples have the right to adopt children?

How do you feel about public versus private school?

How do you like to be taught?

Are you a better teacher or student?

Do you have a mentor? What has this person
taught you?

Have you ever been a mentor? Or tutor? To whom? On
what?

two

Moments in Time
What to ask when you're in a hurry

The high of instant gratification is palpable, especially when we are in the company of someone we physically desire and think we might also be drawn to intellectually and emotionally. That "chemistry" is powerfully alluring and we all want to physically desire our partner, as well we should for a healthy, loving relationship. And we all just can't wait to know what this new person is like sexually. How do they kiss? How do they feel in our arms? What will they be like sexually?

But if I could impart one thing only that would benefit you in your search for a compatible complementary partner, it would be this: slow down sexually until you understand the context of what someone has to offer you. The sex, desire, and lust will still be present once you understand who you are sleeping with—in fact, the desire should grow proportionately to your compatibility as you complement feelings of physical lust with the mental, spiritual, emotional intimacy that develops with them. Recent studies show that on average, Americans become sexually involved by the third date or within six weeks of dating, whichever comes first—usually the third date.

But your understanding of who someone is changes significantly from the first day, week, or month to the sixth month you have known someone. Psychologists report that it takes six months to see if someone's actions are consistent with their words. I disagree with their terminology of "consistent" and replace it with the word *understand*. I believe it takes time, conversations together and shared experiences to fully *understand—moreover, appreciate*—how someone's words are relevant to their actions. This is what I mean by the importance of understanding someone's context and the context of their values.

If he cares, if he is seeking a full, loving relationship and not just a sexual partner, he will wait until you feel that trust, respect, emotional intimacy, and honesty as a foundation to grow your relationship upon before you introduce the additional element of sexual involvement. You may feel you understand who they are and what they have to give you in a month, in five months, in a year. And at the point when you more comprehensively understand who they are, you can decide whether a relationship with them will be healthy for you and if so, if you and he are ready to complement your budding complementary interests and values by including sex and more physical intimacy.

But the time frame is unique to each couple and how your time is spent together. In other words, are you spending time together honestly discussing who you are or spending time doing things you enjoy, but not really exploring beneath the surface? The pace is yours to set. The philosophy of understanding someone's context of what they have to give you and whether they are a compatible partner for you—before you sexually engage with them—is merely to assist you in healthier partnering. It's not meant to punish you into abstinence. It's a philosophy to help you spend your time constantly moving toward happiness and fulfillment and to remove the roller coaster of emotional highs/lows, ups and downs, and insecurities that are an inevitable part of feeling as if you are more emotionally attached/engaged than the person before you. When you physically slow down to understand what they have to give you, you avoid partnering with people who are not capable of giving you what you desire.

Coming in Fast and Furious

I recently completed a large-format art piece called *Get in Line* constructed of cut tin pieces mounted to wood and arranged in a geometric linear pattern. Written on one of the tin pieces is a phrase I think epitomizes how many people approach life: I STAND IN LINE FOR TIME. But this phrase is a paradox: You can't stand in line and get more time, you just have what you have. Time is just an is. As an is, it is present and you are either using it or not. When people meet me, they say, Laurie, it's as if you are . . . eating life, consuming every single minute with a voracious appetite for life.

And yes, that is how I feel, and I have often said I reside at the banquet of life sampling some of everything and returning for seconds on things I relish. One time I asked a boyfriend how we were different. He said, you live life like every day is the last. I thought that was a positive. But after discussing it with him, I realized he thought it was a negative. I have tried to spend my life doing what I love to do all the time; in other words, applying passion to absolutely every element of my life. If I am not enjoying it, then I look for ways to change what I am doing. I always have goals and I am always running headlong toward them. I am not afraid of challenge, difficulty, or failure. I fall and I get up and keep running. People see that I have lots of energy (which I do), lots of passion for what I'm doing (which I do), extreme amounts of ambition (also true), and little or no fear of failing (also true). I think this passion for life must be common to artists or an element of what contributes to a person being creative because I recently watched *Rivers and Tides,* the biography of Andy Goldsworthy. His art is certainly stunning, but what I related to even more was how Goldsworthy incorporated passion, zest, and creativity into every facet of his life. Most people are simply complacent in life, just passing time in activities that don't really capture them soulfully or draw them in with rapture. So, perhaps you're not an artist, but this doesn't mean you can't paint your life full of beauty, and discover all that you are passionate and excited about.

In other words, all you have is time

If you are standing in line for time, you could be missing your life as it passes by you. Run, don't walk, toward your dream. So what does this have to do with asking questions? For me it's simple; I'm on a mission. I want to leave a legacy for the world through writing, art, and the impact I have on my students' lives teaching yoga and after-school self-esteem programs. I want to change the world for the better. I want to give back to humanity. I want to channel my energies into giving. And I want to find someone who is on the same page. I want someone who gets me, isn't fighting me about what I'm doing with my life, how I'm living it. There's a difference between curiosity about what you're doing and just fighting you through the process, out of skepticism or cynicism.

Here's another behavior I've identified: Most people are coasting through life—standing in line for time—and don't feel particularly fulfilled. The secret to happiness is to identify what your particular gifts/talents/skills are, to maximize those qualities in serving something larger than yourself, and to help others discover theirs. Then every day you wake up, you are very focused, and have a deep sense of internal harmony and balance and serenity. Also, the more self-actualized you become, or the more directed and focused on giving and living a compassionate life, the more fulfilled you are personally and the easier it becomes to quickly ascertain if another shares your vision.

When you are trying to ascertain where someone is in their personal development, their ability to communicate, their ability to make peace with their past, then you might discuss any of these:

+ Where are you in life?
+ What are you doing?
+ What was a traumatic experience in your life? Where are you with that now?
+ How do you exemplify honor and integrity?
+ How do you honor the ones you love?
+ How are you giving back?
+ In what ways are you creative?
+ How are you applying your creativity?

The partner whose objective is partnership will desire to know the same of you.

Discuss as you and your partner are comfortable revealing

intimate details about your lives, personalities, and experiences. Remember, it's easy enough to find someone to have dinner with. But it is much more challenging to find a complementary partner. When you start desiring a life partner, someone who resonates on an emotional, intellectual, and spiritual level, then it will become more important to have authentic, soulful conversations about who each of you are. It will become obvious that it's not about interrogating; rather, it's curiosity and understanding that motivates your desire to ask.

Getting to Know Someone at Warp Speed

Some would say, What's the hurry, Laurie? And to that I say, couples should only share what they are comfortable sharing, at the rate they are comfortable sharing. I, personally, have no boundaries, no secrets, so I will share anything from my life, even the most traumatic, most painful experiences, at any stage of when I know someone. When you reach the emotionally healthy place where you can easily discuss even your most painful experiences, then you have reached a place where you can release the control those experiences have over your emotions. A secret is something you are uncomfortable with. But a traumatic experience you can share is just that: traumatic but not controlling of your emotional state of mind.

Secrets or experiences you are unwilling to discuss and share openly are the ones you feel make you vulnerable, the ones you have not internally made peace with. Sharing your life experiences (embarrassing, painful, or some other negative emotion) doesn't make you vulnerable, it empowers you because you release any control the experience has over you by keeping it a secret from the misconstrued belief that it was shameful or wrong. It's an experience, period. We all have them. Learn to discuss it and let it be that, just an experience not a mar on your character.

People who are secretive and very private are not capable of creating deep, intimate, emotional bonds. Do not romanticize their inability to share as mysterious. It's not. It's a sign, a fairly obvious sign, that they have not made peace with themselves. People who are healthy are sharing. They are forthcoming.

I do not judge myself or others. This allows me to share my experiences and listen to others reveal theirs. This doesn't mean I'm a saint without wrongdoing. I'm not. And this doesn't mean I don't have embarrassing experiences or experiences that have been painfully hard to accept about myself. I do. But I know that there's no way to walk forward toward greater enlightenment until I can accept what's happened in the past and admit why I might have acted in a particular way.

People move at their own rhythms and at their own pace for disclosure. And two people may never share at the same pace. It's simply a question, no pun intended, of what draws two people in, what allows them to feel safe, secure, and fulfilled—hence, emotional connectedness. Some are able to do so only sexually. And some are able to do it knowing just the briefest amount of information about another. But I think/feel/believe a deep soulful connection, the connection we (as humans) truly long for, yearn for, comes from a deep understanding of who another person is.

People have their own boundaries. And someone's boundaries of what's off limits in the first hour, first three days, first month, or forever are different. Once you discover what they are, you can either accept that or not, as compatible with who you are and whether you could partner with this person for life or not. But there's no way of knowing what's off limits or what the boundaries are unless you ask what experiences they've had, so you can begin to understand what boundaries they are comfortable with sharing or not.

Do not attempt to mind read and predict what experiences your partner would be comfortable discussing and which ones would leave them uncomfortable. Just ask and let them create the boundaries they are comfortable with. You may assume something about that person that may or may not be accurate, and you may be surprised that something you think might be a deep secret to them because of shame, embarrassment, or sorrow is something they are quite comfortable talking about; on the other hand, some experience that is seemingly trivial to you triggers such great sorrow or uncomfortable emotion in them that they are simply uncomfortable broaching that subject.

Certainly if a man said, Laurie, that was so selfish, egotistical, arrogant, moronic, or whatever other negative judgment he wanted to cast, I would hesitate to share, not because I fear his judgment but *because* judgment is also a sign that someone has not made peace with some part of himself and he feels he has to judge me to make himself feel whole.

Consider the absence of judgment from someone such as the Dalai Lama or typical of some other spiritual figure. They have no judgment. And this suspension of judgment is a quality that is desirable in a partner. When someone judges you it becomes much more difficult for them to accept you, and perhaps impossible to completely accept you. But if someone has no judgment, it's much easier for them to simply accept you for who you are. You are seeking a partner who can support you, knowing that you might trip over yourself sometimes but who can accept you nonetheless.

The greatest human need is self-acceptance—of who we are *as we are*, to be acknowledged, to be validated, to be aware of our existence. Every individual is on her own path of self-discovery, enlightenment, and love.

Unconditional acceptance is just that: unconditional acceptance. It can be frightening and sometimes scary to receive unconditional acceptance from a partner before we have given it to ourselves. Because if you have yet to accept yourself, you fear that the next thing you reveal might alienate them, taking away their love and support.

The Indirect Path

In the broadest overview of men and women partnering, women tend to desire emotional connections first, and men desire sexual connections first. However, to truly be connected we *must* be connected on both dimensions, and I would even include intellectual and spiritual as well. Thus, men and women must work together through conversations toward the objective of finding a soul mate.

But frequently the way men and women pursue a connection to the other places the sexes at odds with one another. It's the rare woman who is so forthright as to admit directly that she desires a partnership. Most women will masquerade their true desire for a lifetime partner by saying they are dating or seeking a boyfriend when what they really desire is a husband.

Men, on the other hand, rarely are honest enough to admit that their first priority is sex. So the sexes dance around one another, each not being completely honest with the other and wondering how they might finagle the experience to give them what they really want.

If you've ever had sex hoping it would turn into a relationship then you understand what I am talking about. And if a man has ever told you he was ready for a relationship only to leave after he had sex, then you really understand what I mean. Women try to lure men to emotional openness and intimacy by becoming physical, and men try to lure women with the promise of "let's get to know one another" through sex.

But in this scenario where two people aren't really honest with one another, both feel tricked into doing something they didn't want: men pressured into a relationship, women pressured into being physical and then feeling like the emotional connections aren't building. Men walk away with even more resolve to not become emotionally intimate in the next relationship. Women sit bereft, hurt, dejected, rejected—feeling as if there's something wrong with them or otherwise the man would have stayed and developed a lasting partnership.

Or the other scenario, where they each find themselves in a relationship that's sort of okay for now, but not very rewarding physically or emotionally. Both tough it out thinking maybe tomorrow it will change, only the two don't have the communication skills in place to admit what they honestly need.

Partner with someone who doesn't share your values and the day you realize this is the day you feel as if you compromised what you desired, wanted, and needed just to be with another person. And when you feel as if you compromised on your happiness, you erode your self-esteem, emotional health, and sense of self. From eroded self-esteem you make other less appropriate decisions, propagating the cycle and downward spiral. Start by asking the right questions.

Top Ten Questions to Ask on a First Date

Are you happy with your career? What if anything would you change?

How old were you when you first fell in love? Who was she?

What is the best compliment I could give you?

Who's the most important person in your life? Why?

What motivates you?

What is your philosophy about life?

Do you wish you had more or less time to see your family?

What book, film, or piece of art inspires you every time you think of it?

Do you consider yourself an analytical or creative thinker, or intuitive? Why?

If you could relive one event in your life what would it be? And how would you redo it?

Questions to Ask When You Only Have a Few Minutes

What are your nonnegotiable rules for a relationship? Such as no yelling, throwing, name-calling, infidelity, violence, saying "shut up," or cussing at a partner?

Do you stay friends with exes?

How do you define love?

If money didn't matter what would you do?

How long would you wait to have sex if you thought you had met your life partner?

Where are you with accepting and loving who you are? All of you? Or just some of you?

What are your favorite qualities about yourself? Physical qualities? Emotional? Spiritual? Intellectual?

If you could remove one problem from the world, what would it be?

What problem would you remove from your
own life?

Questions to Ask to Ignite a Spark

If you had all the time in the world what hidden passions
would you pursue?

Do you kiss on a first date?

What does *soul mate* mean to you?

What do you want to do before you die?

What do you find most alluring about a woman? Her scent,
voice, lips, or other?

How important is physical attraction to you?

How do you like to play? Flirt?

If you could go on one date with any woman, dead or alive,
who would it be and why?

Questions to Ask to Reach Their Soul

What is unforgivable? Before marriage? After?

What makes you feel vulnerable and what makes you feel safe?

Who is your relationship confidante when you can't tell your partner? Why?

What couple do you know that has unconditional lifetime love for the other? In what ways would you like to emulate their partnership?

What is off limits, only to be discussed with your partner?

How do you nurture your partner? Love?

How do you ask for what you need?

Who knows you best?

What do they know that I don't?

Where are you headed? Where have you been? What's around the next bend?

How does marriage make you feel?

Do you have the self-discipline to not become physically involved beyond kissing? How do you know?

What role does physical intimacy have in creating emotional intimacy?

What actions could I do that would make you feel you could trust me?

Do you believe in God or a higher power?

Remember, the more you discuss, the greater understanding and appreciation you have for someone's multifaceted dimensions, and they yours.

three

Aim High
Questions that resonate with passion and purpose

Part of finding a compatible partner is understanding what compatibility looks and feels like. When you understand that compatibility is not characterized by drama, fights, tension, or a feeling that your partner is less than what you wanted or is just okay for now, you can begin to recognize the characteristics of healthy relationships.

Real compatibility is based on acceptance of one another at a core level. You aren't blind to each other's weaknesses or character vulnerabilities; you see them clearly, understand them, understand the context they come from, and can both stand before each other and say, "I don't love you *despite* my seeing these things about you, I love you *because* I understand these quirks and eccentricities. And I accept and love you fully."

From my research and interviews of couples who have enduring marriages of fifty years or more, you might expect that they have common interests, but maybe lack sexual interest or desire for one another. But you would be mistaken. They not only accept my philosophy and believe it, they have been living it for more than fifty years. Their approach is the one I advocate: partner with someone where you share common values, interests, and sexual desire. When I asked them what they argued over during the course of their life together, they laughed in amusement and confessed to the occasional spat where they might have disagreed over something minor such as whether a recalcitrant child should be given additional chores or restricted from leaving the house, but they didn't disagree that the child should be disciplined.

In another instance a couple debated the merits of investing their inheritance in IBM blue chip stock or Southwestern Bell, also a blue chip stock. But they weren't debating about whether to invest the money or spend it; they agreed to invest, it was just a debate of which would provide the biggest dividend. Each adamant that they knew where trends were headed, they decided on an amicable fifty-fifty split applied toward each company. Again, an amicable agreement on something they both fundamentally agreed on: investing and saving for tomorrow.

I heard the couples say repeatedly that for the most part

they agreed on their day-to-day existence as well as the big picture.

In a relationship, you do not have enough time in the day to navigate every single thing that arises. The couples validated this, too, as they said that if they had disagreed on a daily basis, it would have exhausted them and they wouldn't have had any energy to give to themselves or their partner. If they had disagreed on whether to have children, how many to have, or how to raise them, life would have become extremely tedious and odious.

But they viewed life as quite the contrary: as fun, filled with adventure, and yes, hardship and challenge. But they also felt that their spouse was their partner in decisions, best friend in life, mother or father to their children, and lover to the other, and spiritual companion—making life better, easier, and simply more enjoyable because it was shared with the other. This is the kind of commonality you need.

Happily married couples are just that: happy together. They are not complaining about what the partner isn't. They don't spend their time feeling empty, unfulfilled, resentful, or angry at their partner. They celebrate all that their partner is. If you feel the partner you have is lacking more qualities than the amount you appreciate, ask yourself why you're in such a partnership. Do you need to change your attitude about your partner, or change partners? Or a combination of both? Real compatibility exists. It's not what we see portrayed in movies or hawked by the media because melodrama is way more exciting and improbability and chance are marketed as more romantic. But genuine compatibility exists. You must believe it exists for you and that you are worthy of such a relationship and be willing to identify what values you hold dear and are fundamental to your happiness. And you must exhibit the self-discipline to act in accordance with your values and seek another who values the same. And this means being available when the most compatible partner emerges.

Do I have to compromise to get what I want?

I have often heard this question from friends and my column readers. And I say a resounding no! No, you do not need to compromise on the values you seek just to be with another. Here's something to consider, and while this might sound like a riddle, it's not. You can have everything *you* want and value because *you* don't want everything—only what's absolutely most important to you.

Does this seem like a riddle? It's not meant to. Included in this chapter is a list of the most frequently desired qualities we seek in partners. Dr. Neil Clark Warren, clinical psychologist, labels the qualities you want a partner to possess as Must Haves. These are not Desirables, or Hopefully Will Possess Qualities, these are your personality traits that are Must Haves: the ones that must be present in your partner. Some of those will be considerably more important to you than others, in fact absolutely necessary, and those qualities are considered Must Haves as opposed to the opposite—Deal-Breakers, a term I dubbed for a personality quality that is so abhorrent you wouldn't consider a relationship with someone who possesses it.

Many people fear being alone, fear not finding someone, and when that fear dominates their thinking they feel an overwhelming pressure to compromise or settle and partner with someone who is not a good match. Some find themselves in relationships that aren't very gratifying, and when that dissatisfaction becomes impossible to ignore, exit the relationship and start over again. I have certainly done the same in the past—loved someone I knew wasn't really compatible with me and had to leave because it was ultimately unsatisfying.

I am with Lord Alfred Tennyson in that it is definitely better to have loved and lost than never to have loved at all. I only advocate being emotionally smart about your choice of who to give your love to. Are they worthy of it? Will they respect it? Will they honor it? It is one thing to lose a great love at the capricious hands of an unforeseen tragedy, and it is another to lose a love because they couldn't give you what you needed, value you for who you are, or treasure absolutely every day with you.

If you settle just to be with someone, be prepared to settle in terms of happiness as well. But if you can articulate what you want and need from someone, you are well on your way to finding the person who can give it to you.

Does compatibility mean we both like Chinese food, or we both like the missionary position? When you are with someone you are genuinely compatible with, every decision is not provocation for disagreement . . .

How much money you spend on clothes.

Do you eat out or stay in?

How groceries are stored in the pantry.

Do you drive new cars or used cars?

When you share your life with someone, there are far too many details that occur on any given day, much less over a lifetime, to be constantly focused on navigating issue after issue after issue.

The Must Haves: The most highly desirable qualities we'd like to have in our partner. Some of the qualities listed below were identified from Dr. Neil Clark Warren's research on marital satisfaction, and others still came from my talking to couples and singles—some fulfilled and others unfulfilled. Select your partner list by the qualities you most desire in a mate. This is a list comprised of the qualities others find most pleasing about their partners. Review the list and really start to understand what each quality means to you, and how important each one is to your long-term growth and happiness. Here is the list:

EMOTIONAL HEALTH. I must have someone who is emotionally healthy and emotionally stable.

SENSE OF HUMOR. I must have someone who can find humor in life's travails.

STRONG CHARACTER. I must have a partner who is honest and self-empowered and disciplined to do the right thing under the most adverse of situations.

PATIENCE. I must have someone who is tolerant and handles life's challenges with joie de vivre.

TOLERANT. I must have someone who can listen to another's views, empathize even if different from his own, and someone who doesn't need to be right.

ABILITY TO NAVIGATE CONFLICT. I must have someone who is willing and able to navigate/resolve conflicts so that both people feel satisfied with the resolution.

ENERGY LEVEL. I must have someone whose energy level is similar to mine.

EMOTIONALLY GENEROUS. I must have someone who shares affection and empathy verbally.

TRADITIONAL. I must have someone who is traditional regarding sexual needs.

SEXUALLY EXPERIENCED. I must have someone who is sexually experienced, confident, and open to exploration.

PASSIONATE. I must have someone who embraces life and all they do with unbridled passion.

INTELLIGENCE. I must have someone who can engage me intellectually, be it philosophical debates or talking about world issues.

FINANCIAL SECURITY. I must have someone who will be financially responsible.

EMOTIONAL/VERBAL INTIMACY. I must know that my partner is sharing his most honest and intimate feelings, fears, hopes, and dreams.

SELF-CONFIDENT. I must have someone who resolutely believes in himself and draws on an inexhaustible reserve of self-esteem despite life's challenges.

UNASSUMING. I must have someone who can admit if he made an error in judgment, and is able to accept criticism.

ABLE TO ACCEPT HELP. I must have someone who will allow another to help him on important issues.

LOYAL. I must have someone I can always rely on to support me.

ADAPTABLE. I must have someone who is flexible with life's most unpredictable moments.

AUTONOMOUS. I must have a partner who allows me my own space to be my own person.

FAMILY LIFE. I must have someone committed to family, children, and the home we create together.

PERSONAL HABITS. I must have someone who strives for high personal standards of hygiene, fitness, and appearance.

SHARED INTERESTS. I must have someone who shares an interest in what I am passionate about.

INTEREST IN PARENTING AND ABILITY TO DO IT WELL. I must have someone who desires to parent in the same style that I aspire to.

STAYING IN VS. SOCIABILITY. I must have someone who has a compatible need to nest at home and/or socialize with many different types of people.

SPIRITUALITY. I must have someone who is seeking a spiritual path similar to my own.

PERSONALITY. I must have someone whose overall personality I enjoy.

RESPONSIBLE. I must have someone who is able to make moral or rational decisions and therefore answerable for one's behavior; sound in judgment.

RELAXED. I must have someone who doesn't allow life or people to fluster him, someone able to forget about other problems and enjoy the moment.

ATHLETIC. I must have someone who is more than casually interested in athletics.

ADVENTURESOME. I must have someone who embraces the unknown with eagerness, a smile, and is exciting to be around.

KINDNESS. I must have someone who is gentle, tender, and kind.

And the "Ace Card"

Saving Grace

Everyone has a quality/personality trait they believe is a saving grace. My mom has oft told me when I am not exhibiting selflessness in a particular situation, instead of focusing on her frustration with me in that moment, she tries to focus on my saving grace—the one endearing quality that really draws her to me. This quality is someone's saving grace, or their ace card, the quality they exhibit that will make you soften, smile, draw you toward them. Everyone has at least one. My best friend softens when a man exhibits wit and humor. Once you have your list, consider which quality you consider a saving grace and where it falls in importance on your compilation of desirable qualities.

Now create your own Must Have list and resolve to wait for the partner to emerge who is a composite of everything you value—not some of what you value, but all of what you value.

Personality Qualities that Contribute to Relationship Success

Character is the foundation for a healthy relationship. After identifying qualities you'd like your partner to possess, such as athleticism or neatness, also consider these six personality traits as requirements toward building a successful relationship. These are qualities you will want to look for and identify along with your conversations to elicit their other personality traits.

1. Commitment to personal growth
2. Emotional openness
3. Integrity, honesty, sincerity, trustworthiness
4. Maturity and responsibility
5. Healthy self-esteem
6. Positive outlook on life

Questions to Determine Commitment to Personal Growth

What have you learned about yourself emotionally in the past ten years? How has this knowledge helped you to arrive where you are today?

What have you learned from your past relationships and what do you do differently now?

What are your greatest weaknesses? Where do you think they come from?

What sources of help did you use in the past when you or your relationship was in crisis?

Where do you turn to now when you need help?

Questions About Emotional Openness

How do you express your feelings to the people you love?

When you do share your emotions, how do you feel afterwards?

Has an inability to express yourself ever caused problems in your relationships?

If I asked your past partners if you were emotionally open, what would they say?

If I asked your past partners if you were emotionally giving, what would they say?

Questions About Integrity, Honesty, Sincerity, and Trustworthiness

Do you believe partners should share everything? If some things should remain confidential, what would they be?

Have you ever lied to somebody while in a relationship? What caused you to lie? What happened? What would provoke you to do it again?

Did your last partner view you as honest and trustworthy? Why?

What kinds of things do you feel are inherently wrong? What wouldn't bother you? Cheating on income tax, littering, not returning money you found, stealing office supplies, etc.?

How would I know if you were lying? What gives you away?

Questions About Maturity and Responsibility

Are you usually on time or late for your appointments?

In what area of your life would you say you are most irresponsible? Finances, health, returning phone calls, etc.?

Have you been fired from your jobs or have you quit? If you were fired, what were the reasons?

Do you consider yourself sensitive to other people's feelings?

Questions About Self-Esteem

What are you the most proud of in your life?

What kind of emotional abuse or mistreatment have you tolerated in the past? Why did you put up with it? Would you tolerate it now?

What kind of emotional abuse have you inflicted upon someone? How did it make you feel? How did you stop?

What do you do to show love for yourself?

What are your worst health or living habits?

When are you most likely to procrastinate?

What risks have you taken in your life? Are there any risks you have avoided taking?

Questions About Having a Positive Attitude Towards Life

Do you feel people are essentially good, or essentially bad?

When lots of things go wrong at once, how do you react?

What are some of the most important lessons you've learned about sadness in your life?

If you could express your life motto, what would it be?

If you had to explain why the world is the way it is to your children, what would you say?

Do you believe things always turn out for the best? Why?

Questions That Resonate with Passion and Purpose

What adventure do you most long to have?

Who's the most influential person in your life right now?

Are men and women equal?

Would you be your own best friend? If so, what could your best friend do that would make you furious? That would hurt your feelings?

Are men and women more alike than they are different?

Who do you know who is genuinely happy in life? Are you? What makes you happy?

What are your feelings about firearms/weapons? On the job? In the house?

Who do you think is one of the most charismatic figures in contemporary public life?

What's something you absolutely love about living in the United States? In your town/city?

What's something that bugs you about living in the United States? In your town/city?

Who would you describe as being morally reprehensible?

Who do you think is one of the most charismatic figures in history?

How would you respond to public scrutiny?

What have you done that's significant to the world? Is that important to you?

What global issues concern you? Do you have a social responsibility to help these situations? What would you do?

Do you think there's been a decline of morality in America? If so, do you think it's an issue for concern?

If there's been a decline, how do you/we go about resurrecting it?

Do you think it's cultural irony that most people are too embarrassed to broach the subject of condoms, but they'll easily share their bodies with others?

What's an accomplishment you are really proud of?

What religious affiliation do you associate with?

What does your profession/job reflect about you?

What personality quality are you most proud of?

What's something you've wanted to learn but haven't taken the time to?

What's a story from your life you're tired of telling/sharing or explaining?

Who is your favorite couple? Why do you admire their relationship?

Are you where you expected to be at this time in your life?

Who's your biggest fan? Why?

What's on your agenda to do for the next week? Next month, six months, year?

How's your relationship with your opposite sex parent?

What do you think the opposite sex does better? Worse? What annoys you about the opposite sex?

How do you grade the opposite sex overall? And what is a good grade?

Do you owe anyone financially? Emotionally? What's your plan for paying it off?

What negative traits has the opposite sex accused you of? Anger management? Jealousy? Infidelity? Irresponsibility? Being messy? Irresponsible? Selfish? Generous? Flirtatious? Other? What actions on your part triggered your partner to label you?

Who's your best same-sex friend? Why?

Have you ever had or thought about having sex with someone of the same sex? Have you acted upon on it?

Where do you draw the line between changing for another and improving yourself?

Reverse the order: improving, then changing?

How do you adjust to change?

How would you cope if your loved one was wounded, maimed, or disabled?

How would you cope if you didn't know what your loved one's job is, if they could not talk about it, i.e., classified military/law enforcement?

Have you analyzed both sides of a glamorous/dangerous / hazardous profession (e.g., military, law enforcement, firefighting, medical, entertainment, etc.), both the good and the bad? How would you maintain intimacy? Handle extended time separations? Cope with group-ism? Cope with the insular camaraderie?

How long does it take you to get bored by routine?

Do impromptu changes in the evening plans fluster you? If not, what does fluster you?

What's the most traumatic, unanticipated change in life you've had to navigate? How did you do it?

Your date is late. How do you greet him/her at the door? How late does he/she have to be for it to be a problem?

You're running late, what do you do?
    A. Cut prep time in half, not quite assembling the look you wanted but at least you are on time.
    B. Continue at the same pace and forget about being on time.

What has been the greatest change in your life?

What's the greatest change you personally avowed to make and have successfully incorporated into your life?

Fill in the blank: I will never do _____ again. Why? Have you stayed resolved to that mission?

What are you absolutely, under no circumstance, not willing to change for another person?

You come home to find your partner has completely rearranged and edited your household possessions. What do you do?

Your significant other radically changes his/her appearance and literally surprises you at the door. What do you do? What do you say?

Are there set constants in your life that allow you to enjoy spontaneous change in other areas? What are the constants? What are the areas for spontaneity?

Reasons to Ask Before Sex Confuses the Attraction

Are you looking for casual sex or are you at a place in your life where you are open to a long-term relationship?

What would make you committed to our relationship?

What are you prepared to give in terms of time, energy, financial/emotional/spiritual/physical commitment?

What's the foundation of our relationship? Are trust and respect integral elements?

What symbolism/meaning do we each attach to becoming sexually involved?

Have we heard about life experiences from each other that demonstrate a conviction to shared values?

How much do we know of our sexual pasts and the role sex played in our former relationships?

If we don't practice safe sex and we become ill or pregnant, what will we do?

Do we want/value the same things in life across all value sets or just some?

Have we spent time understanding why some past relationships did not progress further?

Do we understand how/why we entered into those relationships at that time in our lives?

What do we each hope to receive from this?

How closely aligned are our perceptions of the world? Do we have a similar frame of reference for interpreting everyday events?

Do we manage our day-to-day lives in a similar fashion?

Do we desire each other with the same intensity?

Do we have a successful ability to manage/talk/negotiate any areas of difference?

Do we have compatible goals for our future together?

For Single Parents

What do you see as your role with my children?

How would you begin to establish a relationship with my children?

How do you raise a happy, confident child?

What qualities of your own would you hope a child would adopt/inherit? Which should they never adopt/inherit?

What do you consider effective nurturing? What about effective discipline?

Dating Coast-to-Coast

What would you be willing to sacrifice for love?
   A. Parents
   B. House
   C. Job
   D. Family
   E. Friends

F. Children

G. Culture

H. Citizenship

I. Other (specify)

If you did leave any of these behind, how would you go about re-creating them in your life to regain balance?

What would you never leave for love?

What's the allure in dating someone who does not live in the same city or state or even same country?

In order to really know someone and what they are like in a day-to-day existence, how do you avoid the oasis effect— when the two of you visit and your regular life responsibilities go on hold during the entertaining and both of you are on your best behavior?

If you were initiating a long-distance relationship, what's the length of time you would be comfortable lapsing between visits?

How do you integrate someone into your day-to-day existence when he or she lives an extensive distance away?

If someone who appeared to be a compatible partner lived in another city, state, or country would that prevent you from getting involved?

If you can't physically be there, how would you comfort your love, celebrate accomplishments, and generally support one another's endeavors?

If you could live anywhere, where would you choose? Why?

How did you come to live where you are now?

How many times have you moved in your life? What prompted those moves?

Where (and how much) are you willing to spend to get to know someone who doesn't live in your vicinity?
   A. DSL/internet connection
   B. Time
   C. Flights
   D. Long distance
   E. Stamps; postage
   F. Other (specify)

Partnering with Diversity

Do you believe opposites attract? Why or why not? What constitutes complementary differences versus too dissimilar to relate?

Do you differentiate between dating someone radically different from your background and marrying someone that different?

What issues would you be willing to accept while dating (as opposed to marrying) someone different from yourself?
    A. Different religion
    B. Different ethnicity
    C. Divorced
    D. Different level of education
    E. Has children
    F. Other (specify)

How different could your date be in that way? Why?

How would you maintain intimacy if you fundamentally disagree?

Have you ever gone somewhere just to do something different? Where did you go and how did it make you feel?

Have you ever done something just to be different? What did you do?

Could you/would you communicate with someone who did not speak your language? How?

What is your comfort zone in terms of difference? What causes you to feel out of your comfort zone?

What's the greatest age difference you'd be comfortable with? Why?

four

The Deal-Breakers
Sex, money, family, and childhood — the answers you need to hear

What Is a Deal-Breaker?

When you select a partner, you are making a decision about someone based on the premise that they come as is—what you see is what you get. Therefore, it's imperative to know not only what are your Must Haves but also the opposite: your Deal-Breakers. What's a Deal-Breaker? Deal-Breakers are the qualities that are intolerable to you; the qualities that you have zero tolerance, zero patience, zero willingness to endure in a relationship. Just as your Must-Have list is important, so is the selection of your Deal-Breakers. There are many qualities that irk and annoy us. They are not Deal-Breakers. A mature adult understands there will be occasions where you think, "I can't believe he just said that or did that." For example, leaving clothes on the floor, dishes in the sink, forgetting to pay a bill, or using incorrect subject/verb agreement in front of your friends—or whatever other personal habit that irks you and makes you roll your eyes to heaven as if to ask for more patience.

A Deal-Breaker is an egregious violation against something you believe or something you value. Racism. Selfishness. Lackadaisical. Financially irresponsible. Slovenly. Just as Must Haves are unique to individuals, so are your Deal-Breakers. What's annoying to me may be amusing to you. What I consider inviolate and absolutely unforgivable, you may consider tolerable. This is another reason why it is imperative to make a list according to you. Your Deal-Breaker List will be gospel according to you. This is not your best friend's list. And not your mom's list.

I cannot give you your list, but I can help you learn how to identify qualities that you would consider unforgivable.

What's the Big Deal About Deal-Breakers, Anyway?

A person's hobbies will come and go, as do the interest and energy they are willing to devote to certain projects. As people grow, change, and mature, their priorities change. And that is to be expected. But a person's values and personality traits endure. You are seeking someone who possesses long-term values and morals that will stand the test of time. And by test of time, I do not mean the first blush of love, nor the first two years of marriage or even seven years of marriage. Everyone talks about wanting a soul mate. We receive thousands of romantic social messages about how we must partner, get married, buy a house together, send our children to summer camp. These messages place an inordinate amount of pressure on dating and relationships. When we don't feel positive about being single and take on the emotional debt or pressures society sends about true happiness coming from marriage, we become desperate to be a part of some other club other than the single one; and the married club becomes fairly enticing just on the merits of escaping our own paradigm. Sometimes we feel rushed into making a decision, and suddenly we find ourselves compromising on what we truly desire in a partner just to have a partner—just to belong to another social club, the emotionally privileged world of being married.

The divorce rate in America is now 60 percent—1.4 in 2. Everyone believes it won't happen to them. But the only way to enduring happiness is to find enduring compatibility.

The Value of a Deal-Breaker

Deal-Breakers destroy love because when someone exhibits something you view as a Deal-Breaker they undermine your love and respect for them. Love and respect are given, not bought. I couldn't make you feel love or respect toward someone. Remember, the foundation of enduring love is respect—not sexual desire.

As I've frequently mentioned, desire is important but it is respect of another's character that will hold your love sacrosanct. I happened to be at my grandparents' house the day before my grandfather had a massive stroke. Only hours before, I sat next to him and my grandmother. They were sitting on the porch swinging. My grandfather leaned over, kissed my grandmother, squeezed her hand, looked at me and said, "I can only try to be more like your grandmother." And her response was, "And me like him." There it was, the secret to their enduring love: after more than forty years of marriage, they both equally respected and admired the other.

Before you make a commitment to someone, think honestly about how you feel about him. Do you like this person? Can you accept him as is? Do you respect him? Do you want to be more like him? When you answer these in the affirmative, you know you've found someone that you genuinely admire.

Most Frequently Cited Deal-Breakers: Qualities We Absolutely Cannot Tolerate in a Partner

+ Lies
+ Cheats
+ Needs to Dominate
+ Financially Irresponsible
+ Unable to Cope Productively with Anger at Others, Self, the World, or Circumstances
+ Interest in Pornography
+ Excessive Drinking or Drug Use
+ Smokes
+ Gambles
+ Sloppy
+ Lazy
+ Procrastinates
+ Gossip

+ Inappropriate Social Behavior
+ Parsimonious
+ Profanity
+ Vain
+ Unable to Achieve Balance in Life—TV Junkie/Golf or Shopping Addict
+ Excessive Weight
+ Judgmental
+ Recklessness
+ Apathetic
+ Infidelity
+ Pessimist
+ Unreliable
+ Intruding Family/ Friends
+ Punctuality/Tardiness
+ Flirtatious

- ✦ Racist
- ✦ Poor Hygiene
- ✦ Hypocritical
- ✦ Self-Centered
- ✦ Victim Mentality
- ✦ Holds Grudges
- ✦ Mean-Spirited
- ✦ Emotionally Immature/ Emotionally Stifled
- ✦ Petty
- ✦ Hypochondriac
- ✦ Discourteous/ Rude
- ✦ Unhappy in Life
- ✦ Obsessive-Compulsive
- ✦ Inability to Admit Wrongdoing or Apologize
- ✦ Lack of Communication
- ✦ Inability to Create Emotional Intimacy
- ✦ Critical
- ✦ Stern
- ✦ Lack of Social Consciousness/ Generosity/Interest
- ✦ Sense of Entitlement
- ✦ Inflexible/Rigid
- ✦ Stoic, Staid, Serious
- ✦ Lack of Self-Awareness
- ✦ Complacent with Life
- ✦ Fear of Risk
- ✦ Obsessively Analytical
- ✦ Wasted/Unutilized Talent
- ✦ Uninterested in Growth
- ✦ Staunchly Independent
- ✦ Righteous
- ✦ Politically Unaware
- ✦ Clumsy
- ✦ Sexually Inept
- ✦ Unhappy with Immediate Family
- ✦ Materialistic
- ✦ Denies Self-Responsibility
- ✦ Workaholic
- ✦ Worrier
- ✦ Co-Dependent
- ✦ Arrogant
- ✦ Extreme Shyness

- Religious Incompatibility
- Spiritually Intolerant
- Spiritually Indifferent
- Boorishness
- Extreme Focus on Political Correctness
- Reckless Driver
- Fanatical
- Divorced
- Bi-sexual Intolerance
- Pet or animal cruelty

Every person has her own list of things that are *absolutely,* under no condition, even remotely tolerable. After you work through this list, you will have an even better understanding of yourself. Your heightened sense of enlightenment about what you could tolerate versus what you could forgive will put you closer to the purity of love you are seeking. No one said that making lists was a quick process. If this process didn't require you to take some time out and really think about your answers, everyone would be making lists and more people would be in lasting relationships rather than finding themselves in dead-end relationships time and again.

Denial Is a River in Egypt and a Thought in My Mind

When we like someone, there is a huge temptation to ignore something that we don't want to see. Suffice to say that if something feels a little off, or something between you just isn't quite resonating, spend more time talking about it. And allow yourself the time to accumulate enough experiences to understand where the uneasy feeling stems from. I'm not suggesting a big game of Aha: Caught You! but more of an understanding of where your anxiousness originates. We aren't mind readers. But if you pride yourself on having intuition about people and situations, listen to it and just move cautiously. Don't ignore the feeling, hoping it will go away. Yes, it might go away. But if you have reservations about someone's ability to be faithful, trustworthy, and honest in the way you desire, do not set yourself up for the disappointment by discovering it after the fact, after he betrays you with some action that is really hurtful.

There is no gratification in someone else saying "I told you so." But there's damn sure no satisfaction by telling yourself, "I knew it. I knew inside that he couldn't be trusted." Discovering after the fact that you were astute enough to sense a quality about your partner that made you uncomfortable, but were too impatient to move cautiously, is like being hit twice for the same thing.

We all have stories of 20/20 hindsight, myself included. It would be hard to have exposed ourselves to the joys and vulnerabilities that accompany love without also exposing ourselves to the pitfall of denial at some time or another. What separates one experience from another is some of these experiences have been more excruciating because they cost us more—more in time, more in terms of the blow we took to our self-esteem, more even in terms of financial jeopardy. But they all end the same: Loss.

Do People Lie?

What is lying? People occasionally fib and sometimes embellish, but lying is pretty harsh. A lie implies intentional deceit. Of all the men I've dated, I only dated one person who I discovered had been diagnosed as a sociopathic liar. The rest just portrayed aspects of themselves from the context of their reality and their experiences.

Most people intend to present their best face, and would like you to think the best of them. Sometimes, in our eagerness to "connect," we project onto people what we hope they mean. And when our interpretation contradicts their interpretation, we assume they lied to us. They didn't. They just have had different experiences than ours and define their world differently than we do.

In dating, we frequently assume our meaning of words is the same as someone else's, but this is where we find ourselves in a meaning conundrum when we realize a potential partner meant something else entirely when he said. . . . financial stability. . . . recreational drugs . . . available . . . seeking commitment . . . managing debt . . . etc. Thus, we are quick to call someone a liar when our experiences lead us to define the value differently than they do. But they are not necessarily liars. They are just talking from their context of experiences and it's up to you to ask around the subject to discover what they mean.

Driving Through Someone's Life

In our zealous desire to save time and either enter a relationship quickly or leave a relationship that has no long-term promise, we categorize people into genres of acceptability, and therein lies the expanse of misinterpretation.

Sitting in the Love Drive-Thru, we order by number—Number One: Desire to Parent. Number Two: Stability. Number Three: Ambitious. Yet we're shocked, chagrined, angry, hurt, confused, and disappointed when we get home and realize that although we ordered our favorite burger and fries—even upsized it all to a good lover—what we got was a one-night stand.

So how do we avoid becoming a casualty of Fast Food Love? Initiate conversation that encourages more than a yes or no answer. I call this asking around a subject. When you ask in this way, you give someone an opportunity to expand and tell a story, a story that includes more than "Yes, I am physically active," or "No, I never go to the gym."

An important but often overlooked aspect of someone's present state of mind is his current and past relationship with parents, because the relationship an adult fosters with his parents reveals a lot about childhood wounds and whether they've been repaired. It also gives you insight as to what they believe is good parenting.

Compare the question "Do you like your parents?" with the ones below and see how the latter opens the door to hearing stories about someone's life, stories where they can elaborate about who they are and how they adopted certain tenets as truths for right and wrong, good and bad.

+ Whom do you more closely resemble physically (and emotionally), your mom or dad? How so?
+ What was the most valuable lesson your parents tried to teach you?
+ What's a favorite childhood memory with your mom (and dad) that always makes you smile?
+ How old were you when you learned the truth about Santa or Tooth Fairy? How did you respond?

Even if you share a lot, and even if your frame of reference is much the same for most everything, there will be topics where your experiences in life differ, where you have processed hurt, sadness, disappointment, anger, disillusionment, joy, and eagerness differently.

So before you scream "Liar!" and haul out the polygraph, try to understand someone's context.

Evaluate Your Deal-Breaker List

Evaluate what's on your list. And then ask yourself honestly how many of those qualities you possess. Do you possess any? Even one of them? Are you asking someone to eradicate a negative trait that you haven't dealt with in yourself? The Deal-Breaker list works just like the Must-Have list from chapter 3. If you can't ask someone to be something you're not, it stands to reason, you can't ask someone to *not* be something that you are.

All people have idiosyncrasies. Some are more intolerable than others. Know what you're signing up for and understand that complexity before you say, "Yes, let's sleep together," or "Yes, I am committed to you." To love someone is to understand him in all his complexity and it also means absolute acceptance of everything about him—the glowing attributes and the not-so-sparkling traits. When you fully accept someone, you reframe your thinking and you don't view weaknesses as faults, but as qualities that make him real, because you understand where the context of that vulnerability comes from and you are actually more protective of him when that trait surfaces. When a less-than-lustrous quality emerges, and you wholly accept and love someone, you don't pounce on him with an "Aha! A weakness for me to scorn and judge." Loving and wholly accepting another means you come to him with compassion. You don't necessarily have to celebrate his vulnerabilities, but you do approach him with unconditional compassion. You help him strive for greater understanding of himself and hopefully help him find greater strengths within himself.

Fatal Flaws

A fatal flaw is a personality trait that would hinder someone from developing a healthy, emotionally intimate relationship. Fatal flaws are hard to identify and admit if you become prematurely emotional or sexually involved with a new partner.

Therefore, you want to ask questions to identify all aspects of someone's personality prior to emotional attachment. Recognizing fatal flaws and extricating yourself early will help you avoid frustration and discouragement that can hinder your personal growth, and help you better allocate your time and energy.

Fatal flaws are only fatal if you don't face them and let them become building blocks on the road toward intimacy. Thus, if someone is willing to admit to a personal vulnerability and you are willing to spend the time with him to see if he can work through it, it's possible you can form a healthy relationship. But you also need to be aware that you might spend the time with him only to discover that he cannot or will not change that aspect of himself.

Remember that flaws are only fatal if someone doesn't face and conquer them. They can be opportunities to grow in humility and betterness, not pride and bitterness. And they can become building blocks as opposed to dividing walls.

The Deal-Breakers

Sex, Desire, and Eroticism

How did you learn about sex? About love?

Have you ever been married? Divorced?

Do you have any children? If yes, in or out of wedlock?

Do you look into someone's eyes when you make love?

What takes your breath away?

What—of yourself—are you saving for your soul mate?

Do you lose yourself when you get involved with someone?

Is monogamy necessary to you?

What circumstances have led you or would lead you to betray a vow of monogamy?

How do you define infidelity?

Have you ever betrayed a lover? Emotionally? Sexually? Is there a difference to you?

What does your ideal relationship look like?

What are the different types of love you have felt and how would you define them?

How do you show love?

What compromises and sacrifices are you willing to make in the name of love?

What's your favorite kind of kiss?

If you could have just one kiss from your lover, where would you want it?

What is your favorite time of day to make love?

How many times a week would you like to make love?

What is your least favorite part of your body?

Where do you most like to be touched? How?

Do you make love with the lights on?

Have you ever said, "I love you," because you thought the other person expected to hear it?

Do you have that certain feeling when you see your lover walk through the door?

Has someone ever flirted with you that you didn't act on and you wish you had?

How do you flirt?

Do you flirt with your lover? How? In a group or public setting? When it's just the two of you?

When is the right time to become sexually involved?

How many times have you been in love? Who were your lovers?

What's the relevance in your life to the number of times you've been in love?

Can you arouse your lover without touching her?

Blindfolded, can you recognize your lover by smell?
Touch?

What's the first place you touch your lover? Do you do it
the same every time?

Do you like to boast about your partner's accomplishments
or sexual acts with you?

What's sacrosanct between a couple and therefore off limits
to share with anyone else? What type of information do
you feel is appropriate to share with your family and
friends?

When was the last time someone seduced you with charm?
Body? Mind?

Can you succumb to the pleasure of letting go?

Do you feel closer or more distant after making love to
someone for the first time?

How do you refer to your exes? How would they describe
you?

What do your former loves have in common?

What do they have in common with yourself?

Would you rather be sexually or intellectually attracted to another?

Do you know what STD means?

Do you ask a lover if he's tested negative? For which diseases? Do you trust your partner to tell the truth or do you ask for tangible proof? Would you be willing to share your own paperwork?

If someone tested positive for something, how would that affect your decision to become involved? Would that be an immediate deal-breaker, even if you were in love?

How long does it take you to learn your way around a new lover?

What do you like better?
   A. Kissing
   B. Foreplay
   C. Hard-core sex
   D. Other (specify)

How do you like to be kissed?

    A. Deep

    B. Soft

    C. Bitten

    D. Hard and rough

Is orgasm the beginning, middle, or end of sex for you?

How do you broach the subject of your lover's sexual technique and whether it's "getting the job done"?

What do you think is erotic? Neurotic?

Has a lover ever shocked you with a specific request? What was it?

Do men have realistic expectations for women's bodies? For aging? How do magazines such as *Maxim* affect those views?

Is it a partner's job to make the other feel comfortable with herself and the interplay between you two? Or is it up to each individual? Where do the lines cross, if at all?

How do you draw your lover out (i.e., make her feel completely comfortable with you)? With her body? With whatever you two are doing together?

What's the most alluring thing your partner can do to turn you on? To relax you?

What's your tolerance in a partner's weight gain before it begins to turn you off? Five pounds? Ten? Twenty? Fifty? Does it not matter if your lover gains weight? And if he or she is heavy, does it matter as long as he or she is healthy?

Are you consistently drawn to the same kind of physical appearance? What kind of physique?

Does wearing sexy underwear make you feel sexy?

Do you feel sexy in whatever you're wearing?

What could someone do/say to make you feel sexy?

Has someone ever taken your breath away just by looking at you?

Are you nervous under the forthright gaze of another?

Is it easier for you to say, This is what I need from you as a lover or, This is what I need from you emotionally?

Do you think of yourself as . . .

    A. sexually open

    B. adventurous

    C. curious

    D. traditional

In what ways?

Do you punish a lover when you are angry?

Do you:

    A. show disappointment

    B. show you are hurt

    C. withhold sex

    D. withhold conversation

Would you feel comfortable caressing yourself in front of your lover?

Would you feel comfortable watching your lover caress herself?

How do you know if you're coming to someone out of need or want? What's healthy?

What do you love about women?

What do you love about men?

How old were you when you received your first real kiss?
Who kissed you? Did you like it?

Was your first time to have sex an act of love or curiosity?
Did you enjoy it? Did your partner?

What do you know about pleasing a partner?

Women's orgasm: whose responsibility? The man's?
Or the woman's?

How old were you on your first time?

Who taught you the most about making love? What did
you learn?

How well do you remember the first time?

Have you ever felt sexually taken advantage of? When?
Why?

When was the first time you felt like a
woman/man?

When your lover walks through the door, what's the first
thing you say or do?

At a restaurant, your lover leans over and tells you there's food stuck in your teeth. Are you filled with relief or embarrassment?

Have you ever told someone, "I'm not physically attracted to you?" How did they react?

Has someone ever told you they didn't find you attractive? How'd you handle it?

What's your recipe for Love Potion #9?

What is your idea of a romantic evening?

Could you imagine a marriage where you and your partner have separate bedrooms? Separate residences?

On first sight, what qualities motivate you to remember someone?

What piques your curiosity?

What awakens your desire?

Do you derive the greatest sexual pleasure from giving or receiving?

What have you adored about past lovers?

How many lovers have you had? How many were one-night stands? How many lasted a week to one month? How many lasted one month to six months? How many were longer term? How long?

What is the longest length of time you were involved in a relationship?

What does it mean to be attracted to someone's essence?

What is the essence that holds the greatest allure for you?

Would you rather see your lover already dressed for an evening out or watch her get ready?

Have you ever been pleasantly surprised by a lover? Unpleasantly surprised? How? Why?

Have you ever been surprised by a lover's confession? What caught you off guard? What was your response?

If you were at a party and someone of the opposite sex came up to you and said, "I can give you everything you're not getting in your current relationship," what would you say? What would you do? What are you not getting?

Could you connect with what was making you unhappy? Would you tell your partner that you were unhappy? Would you vow to find it in your existing relationship? Or would you be tempted to find it with a stranger?

What do you think is sexy?

Would you rather be thought of as sexy or smart?

When you want to feel sexy what do you wear or do?

What is good sex?

Do you always practice safe sex? If not, why not or when?

Do you demand someone use a condom or do you request it?

How do you bring up the subject of condoms or other contraceptives with a new partner?

Do you have a funny or serious line? What is it?

How do men and women view sex differently?

Do you differentiate between making love and having sex? If so, how?

How would you feel if someone said, "Look, I'm not interested in a relationship with you, but if you want to have sex . . . ?"

Who taught you about the opposite sex? What did they teach you?

What ramifications do those lessons have on your adult life?

Have you ever been able to duplicate your best sexual experience?

Have you ever stayed in a relationship too long because the sex was really good?

Who is responsible for birth control, the man or the woman? Why?

How do you know when you really know your partner?

Where do you stand on the issue of sharing sexual history? How much do you share?

How do you know when to become sexually involved?

How old were you before you could talk about sex and not get embarrassed?

In the past, what was your secret sign or secret code for "I want you?" Or for "Let's ditch this party and head home—now!"

Do you have a code now? What is it?

How important is physical attraction when you are searching for a partner?

Do you believe in love at first sight? Or is it lust?

What's the longest you've been willing to wait before consummating your passion? Your love?

Have you ever known it was the last time at the time it was occurring? How did it make you feel?

Is chocolate a substitute for sex with a partner? Is anything? If so, what?

How do you feel about premarital sexual liaisons?

What's your biggest personality challenge in a relationship?

How much sex do you need a week to feel fulfilled?

Money

How is your financial health?

What does money mean to you?

Are you a saver or a spender? In what areas?

Do you gamble? In casinos? In the stock market?

What do you throw money away on?

Do you overdraw your bank account? For what reasons?

How would you get yourself out of a financial predicament?

How would you recover from financial ruin? What does financial ruin mean to you?

Do you balance your checkbook? How often? To the nearest hundred? Nearest ten? To the penny?

What's the future of the futures market? The stock market?

If someone gave you an insider trading secret, would you use it to make money?

When would you loan money to a friend? A lover?

Who is more likely to ask you for money? Lover? Friend? Family? Ex? IRS? Credit card? Attorney? Doctor? Other?

When would you feel comfortable accepting money as a gift?

If you received $25,000, what would you do with it?

Do you carry cash or credit cards?

What's your credit limit? Emotionally? Financially? Is it maxed out? If yes, was it worth it?

How do your spending habits reflect your values?

Would you prefer to buy one of the very best of something or several moderately-priced items?

When you marry, will you have two separate accounts, one joint account, or all three?

What outstanding debts do you have? How long until you hope to fully pay them off?

What does the greatest percentage of your money go toward?

How much of your retirement have you accumulated already?

Would you take a chance on a high-risk/high-return investment to retire ten years earlier, or would you play it safe?

Have you ever bought a lottery ticket? What were you hoping to buy if you won?

How much money do you need to be happy? Weekly? Monthly? Annually? Lifetime?

Family

Are your parents still alive? What about your grandparents?

Are/were your parents soul mates? What about your grandparents?

Do your parents hold hands? Did they ever?

Do they kiss/show affection in front of the children?

Where does your family live? How often do you see them?

How often do you talk to your parents? To your grandparents?

Are you someone's father/mother? aunt/uncle? cousin? godmother/godfather? grandparent?

Who was your favorite relative growing up? Why?

What qualities did you adopt from your parents that you value? That you detest?

Do you have siblings? How many? Which sibling do you least get along with? Which sibling do you most respect?

Where are you in the family? Oldest? Youngest? Middle?

Do you think your parents did a good job raising you? Why?

What have your parents criticized in your past? Does it still bother you?

Do your parents criticize you now as an adult? If so, what is it for?

What events/actions have ever strained your familial relationships?

Are you more like your mother or your father?

Who do you wish you were more like? Why?

Was your mother a nurturer?

Do you want to have children? Why?

Are you scared of being a parent? Are you afraid you'll make a mistake?

What is your biggest fear of parenthood?

What's the most important lesson you hope to impart to your children?

What are your three wishes for your children?

What kind of parent do you want to be?

How much time can/will you dedicate to parenting?

Are you more interested in being the primary care provider or breadwinner?

What is your emotional remedy for a sick/sad/angry child?

Have you ever defied your parents' wishes?

Have you lived up to your parents' expectations? To your own expectations?

How has a woman's role evolved since you were a child? A man's role?

What's the most appealing kind of marriage to you?
    A. Traditional
    B. Egalitarian
    C. Open
    D. Something else (specify)

What household responsibilities would you like to handle?

What household responsibilities would you like your partner to handle?

What do you want someone else to handle while you retain veto power?

Up to what age would you consider having a child?

If you could know the gender of your child, would you want to?

What's your heritage?

What family traditions did you love that you would like to carry on in?

Which ones would you like to forget about?

What's an experience you shared with your grandmother that makes you giggle whenever you remember it? How about your grandfather?

What did you call your grandmother? Your grandfather?

Did you ever call your parents by their first names?

What did your family argue about? What do they argue about now?

How did your parents encourage you to get along? What did you learn from that?

Did your parents fight in front of the children? Do they now? Did it bother you if they did? Does it bother you now?

What did your parents teach you about navigating conflict?

Did you take family vacations as a child? Where?

When your family traveled, how did they go?

What's the first adjective your family would use to describe you?

What do you think your parents did right/good in their marriage? Was it unique to their situation/personality or would you like to adopt it as well?

Have you or a significant other ever had an abortion? Under what circumstances?

What would you do if you and your partner were pregnant and amniocentesis revealed birth defects?

Would you ever adopt a child? Under what circumstances? Of another race? With disabilities?

How would you respond if your child announced he or she was gay?

How would your parents handle a child who was gay?

Who's your least favorite person in your family?

Are either of your parents your best friend? Or confidante?

What would you like to change about your relationship with your parents?

If there were something you could change about your parents what would it be?

What requirements should we have to fulfill before we get married? Or have children?

Do you believe in naming children after inanimate objects, such as Moonbeam or Apple?

Would you name a child after a favorite sports figure, rock star, or other famous person?

Childhood

Did you feel loved and accepted as a child?

What's your best memory from childhood?

What's a childhood memory that still tugs at your heart?

What's a childhood memory that always makes you smile?

Where did you spend your childhood? Would you like to return?

Did you ever run away from home as a child? Why? Where did you go?

What was your best subject in school?

Did you have any pets when you were a child? What were they? What were their names?

Did you go to camp as a kid? What kind?

Did the kids at school make fun of you? What for? Did you get over it? How?

Did you have braces as a kid?

What was your favorite toy as a child?

What is your favorite toy as an adult?

What did you always want as a child that your parents would never let you have? Did you ever get it for yourself?

Did you ever get sent to the principal's office?

What is the one thing that consistently got you in trouble at school? With your teachers? With your parents? With your classmates?

What's the most valuable class you took in high school? Beyond?

Where did you go to school? Do you wish you'd gone somewhere else?

Did you ever have an imaginary play friend? Do you remember when he/she left your life?

What responsibilities/chores around the house were yours as a child?

How has that served you later as an adult? Are you still responsible?

Were you the popular kid?

Are you the popular adult?

Were you the first one picked for the baseball team, or the last?

How were you disciplined as a child? Was it effective?

As a child, did you sleep with a nightlight? What's your adult equivalent?

What generation American are you?

Did you have your own room as a child?

What food did your mom forbid you to have as a child? Do you still crave it? Do you eat it now?

What food did your mom let you have if you were really good? Do you still crave it? Do you eat it now?

What was your favorite Halloween costume as a child? Was it purchased or made? By whom?

What's your favorite Halloween costume as an adult?

How old were you when you learned to ride a bike? Who taught you?

Did you ever have a babysitter or nanny as a child? Did you like her? If so, what did you like specifically?

Ever have a crush on a teacher? If yes, what grades? Why?

Did you have one teacher who inspired you beyond all the others? Was it someone who saw your greatness before you did, and who told you? Are you in contact with that person today?

What was your favorite childhood game? Why?

What was your favorite childhood story? Why?

What kind of music did your parents listen to? Do you still listen to it? How does it make you feel?

What one song from childhood or your youth do you remember that still makes you soften today? Why does it make you soften?

As a kid, did you play Cowboys and Indians? Were you the Cowboy or the Indian? Did you play Tarzan and Jane? Were you Tarzan or Jane?

As a kid, what did you think you wanted to be when you grew up? Have you become that?

What smell takes you back to childhood?

What right of passage claimed your childhood innocence? If you could do it over, would you do it the same way?

five

Personalities Collide
How important are lifestyle and compatibility?

I used to think the idea of dating my opposite was fun and romantic. But it's not. It's obnoxious. I am neat and organized and I like my house that way. I am a high-energy athlete and I like moving at that pace. I am ambitious and willing to work long hours to achieve my goals. I'm an artist and I can spend hours doing cultural things, and I have no interest in football. I like dating someone like me. I used to think if I dated someone who walked through life, it would slow my run down. Then I realized I don't want to walk through life; I love bounding through life.

The allure of opposites is appealing only until you realize your values. At that point it's just annoying. You can have differences but you can't have less respect for them because they are different. You can like different things as long as you don't feel superior to them. Your relationship can exist with personality and lifestyle differences as long as when you indulge someone's differences it doesn't make you angry or resentful. When overcoming your differences begins to feel like work, then you know you've partnered with someone who may be more different than you can handle comfortably.

This is where you really use your Must-Have and Deal-Breaker lists. If you have satisfied your Must-Haves and are fortunate enough that your partner doesn't possess a Deal-Breaker, then roll with the difference and get creative in navigating toward one another. If you love to travel to Europe and she can't stand to leave the United States, find the most European city in the United States and go. Or explore what it is about European travel you love. I enjoy being out of the American culture, so for me to simulate that experience in the United States would mean placing myself in a remote location unlike something I've experienced . . . say, Alaska.

If your core values align and you don't possess a Deal-Breaker, you will find that it's much easier to communicate and resolve the seemingly smaller issues that arise or experiences that lead to outcomes where you disagree. But you have to start with core values and work to the smaller differences. If you have great sex and nothing else, then you have nothing else. If you have all your values in common but different frequency needs for sex, get creative with your physical expressions of desire such that making love includes more than just the physical.

Everything you don't agree on has to be negotiated. It certainly can't be ignored and there's a limited amount of time you can spend negotiating. Major issues or core values take a long time to negotiate because, frequently, there isn't a middle ground because you do feel so passionate about the issue or value being discussed. Smaller differences really can be inconsequential and can be navigated.

Another insight by psychologists who've studied couple compatibility: Couples *can* be vastly different and still perceive the relationship a success *if* they can focus on the positives of the relationship or what they have in common. When you have everything in common, you don't have to focus on the positive because it's inherent in the relationship. But you can learn to focus on what you have in common even if you do have a few dissimilarities. It's still all mind-set. It's easier if you have more in common, but not impossible if you don't. It just requires more work and a larger change of mind-set.

General Lifestyle

How would you cope if you and your lover were on different work/sleep schedules for an extended period of time?

Would you describe yourself as a physically hyperactive or as a low-key person?

Is love need-based or want-based?

Would you write your own wedding vows? What would you say?

Do you think love is simple or complex?

Are mental gymnastics titillating or annoying?

Are you at your heaviest, ideal, or thinnest weight right now? Do you think you look better now or five years ago?

Who is responsible for making the first move? And what should the first move be?

What grates on your nerves in a lover?

Do you believe in love at first sight? Have you ever felt anything like that?

How are you romantic?

Do you have a favorite side of the bed?

Do you like to spoon?

What do you sleep in?

If your lover brought you something sexy to wear to bed, what would it be?

What bedtime story would you tell me? Would it be fact or fiction?

If someone could tell you whom you'd marry, would you want to know?

If I could look into your future and tell you that you were to spend your life unmarried, what would you say?

Have you ever fallen in love with someone from another race? If not, why not? If yes, would you/did you pursue it?

Do you get irritated with people who misplace things?

How much affection do you like? Physical? Verbal? What do you reserve for a lover only?

What are three fatal flaws that would nix a relationship almost immediately?

What's the best thing someone can do for you (and for herself) when you're on a tirade or in a funk?

Define your personal space. What do you do when someone invades it? Emotionally? Physically?

What is the kindest or most beautiful gesture a friend could offer you?

Are you a lover or a fighter?

Do you think people who seek therapy are weak?
If so, why?

How much sleep do you need to be highly productive?

What would a very active weekend day look like? An average day?

Have you ever done drugs? Which ones?

Do you live alone, with a roommate, or with your parents?

Are you a cat or dog person? Is that preference from childhood?

Are you a toll tag person? Or do you have the change prepared ahead of time? Or do you scrounge for change as you sit at the tollbooth? Or run the toll altogether?

Do plants prosper under your nurturing hands? What else do you nurture?

If you were to plant a garden, what would you plant?

Where have you traveled?

How do you travel?

When you travel, do you prefer a tour guide or self-guided tour?

You're traveling in Europe and your backpack, wallet, credit cards, cash, and passport are stolen. How do you respond? What do you do?

How many glasses of wine does it take for you to lose your sense? How does that make you feel?

Do you remember jokes?

Have you ever been in jail, in any country?

What are your hobbies?

Do you drink coffee?

How do you make your coffee—do you measure with precision or just pour with approximation?

What kind of coffee do you drink? How much do you drink in a day?

In the morning, do you bring coffee to bed? Do you like your lover to bring it to you? Where?

Are you a morning person or a night owl?

Are you neat or messy?

Do you prefer big soirees or tête-à-tête birthday parties?

Do you read the financial pages? The funnies? Your horoscope? Which one do you read first?

Do you prefer a shower or bath?

Where do you sit when you ride on roller coasters? Front? Back? Middle? Or elect not to ride at all?

Do you sing along when you hear a song you like?

Can you whistle? Do you whistle?

Are you an organ donor?

Have you ever been involved in a car accident? Was it your fault? Were there injuries? To whom?

Have you ever had a DUI?

Have you ever gotten a speeding ticket?

Do you like to talk on the phone? Or do you prefer to write letters? Or do you prefer email?

Is long-distance telephone service a luxury or a necessity? Is information a luxury?

Health

How would you describe your health?

How's your physical shape?

Have you broken any bones? How? Which ones?

Do you exercise? How often? What method of exercise do you pursue?

How fast can you ascend three flights of stairs? Does it leave you winded?

Would hang gliding the Grand Canyon scare you or thrill you?

How long can you hold your breath?

Can you swim? Do you like to swim?

What's the most physically grueling thing you have ever subjected your body to? Would you do it again?

How much weight have you gained since high school? Where did it end up? Do you care to work at losing it?

Have you lost any weight since high school? How much?

What's a sport you revere but wouldn't attempt to master?

What's a sport that bores you?

Exactly how far can you bend? Can you touch your toes?

When traveling, do you find a place to work out?

How important is your health? What do you do to maintain/improve your health?

How long did your grandparents live?

What are you not willing to sacrifice just to live longer?

Do you diet? Do you ever fast?

Have you ever been addicted to some substance? (Chocolate excluded!)

Are you still struggling with any addictions? What are you doing about it?

How's your mental/emotional health?

Have you ever sought therapy? For what? Did it work?

How do you measure the success or failure of therapy?

Do you believe in hypnosis? Have you ever been hypnotized? If yes, for what purpose?

Do you believe in acupuncture? If yes, have you used it? What for?

What's your best sport?

Do you do anything athletic that requires equipment or athletic finesse? How good are you at it?

Are you claustrophic? Afraid of heights? Any fears/phobias?

What are you allergic to? What does it do to your system/body? Is the allergy life-threatening?

If somebody said, Take this drug, there are no lasting effects, no temporary or permanent damage, no one will ever know, and it will make you feel more wonderful than you've ever felt before, would you take the drug?

What gives you that same feeling naturally?

Have you ever experienced a runner's high? An athletic high in any sport?

six

The Truth Revealed
What to ask about past relationships and behavior patterns

Our generation has learned well the categorical ability to compartmentalize emotions, sexuality, and soulfulness, thus giving rise to the cultural norm and acceptance of casual sex, bootie calls, friends with benefits, and the idea of "we're just fk'g, we're not involved," all the while really confusing the definition of what making love really means and who really is making love.

When you become so efficient at dividing your sexuality from your emotions, you are eroding the union of the mind, body, and soul such that when you desire to emotionally connect with someone you are simply unable to—all you know is how to be physically naked, and not present with the other. Our generation of singles has adopted casual sex as acceptable behavior. Consider these questions:

How much superficial sex do you need?

How many orgasms do you need from different partners who don't have a vested emotional, intellectual, spiritual interest in you or your well-being? In other words, what's enough before you grow tired of superficiality and want something more or different?

What does your willing participation in superficial relationships say about your own sense of self-respect? In other words, do you not feel you are worthy of more from a partner? And do not kid yourself by saying casual sex is all you want and that's what you're getting. That's what you tell yourself when you are afraid to admit you want more and afraid you might not find it, so you compromise yourself and your own happiness, trying to fill the loneliness with superficial sex.

What do you consider is the foundation for a healthy, fulfilling relationship? And how does that align with how you are creating relationships? What do you suppose is preventing you from creating a healthy, loving relationship?

The ability to honestly engage another and develop genuine intimacy is a sign of emotional health. Despite the media, social, and cultural messages we've received, it is not emotionally healthy nor empowering to be able to objectify people, remove yourself emotionally from an experience such that only your body is engaging in the interaction. *This is not healthy.*

We repeat experiences in our lives until we take the time to understand how they affect us and consciously *decide* to do it differently next time. Until that moment of epiphany, we continue to run the same patterns because it feels comfortable, because it's what we know. Thus, superficial sex over and over, or even superficial relationships that start quickly and end quickly, do not set a precedent for showing you how to engage another on an authentic level. It only reinforces objectification of people, categorization of your emotions, and the most banal and superficial of relationships.

I believe our generation has learned to say and think that it's cool, and even hip, to have relationships that are characterized as "We're just f**king." And I think there are both men and women who believe this. But, I believe that men and women who say they are content to just have sex sans any emotional development *are not* in an emotionally healthy place. Casual sex breeds selfishness and selfishness is the demise of genuine, honest, compassionate, emotionally revealing love.

Despite how you or someone you are potentially involved with has lived their life up to this point, you can move toward a higher state of awareness and giving. In essence, it is possible—and very doable when you consciously elect to reunite your mind, body, and soul. Emotional nakedness is just that: the ability to be physically naked *and* emotionally naked, comfortable revealing your biggest fears, insecurities, and failures while extending yourself to trust another, to care about another, to accept him without judgment.

This is what emotional sexual honesty is. And just because you have sex with someone does not mean they are capable of becoming emotionally naked with you. While the reverse is true: if someone is willing to be emotionally naked with you, they are much more likely to be willing to be physically naked with you, and the act of physical involvement then intensifies your emotional connectedness.

You want to partner with someone who is extremely emotionally healthy. And you must learn to recognize who can emotionally engage in loving emotions. Some people can. And others can't. Thus, the necessity of asking questions and engaging in conversation prior to giving yourself sexually. Conversation allows you to elicit where someone is and decide whether or not they will be able to emotionally engage with you. You are not making a judgment on where they are in their life, or what they have to give you. You are simply observing it and deciding whether you are compatible with it or not. Through conversation, you can elicit what a potential partner is capable of giving, and what they desire from life and, potentially, a relationship with you.

When I talk with someone, I find it very easy to ascertain where he is in life and emotional development. Sometimes I have encountered someone who I wanted to change so that he could be farther along in his emotional development, but people are where they are. And they have to *want* to develop to the next state of awareness; not because you desire them to be there, but because they realize the mental health benefits of greater awareness.

As a rule: *DO not go to bed or become physical with someone until he is comfortable enough revealing his biggest insecurities.*

If you ask why insecurities, it's simple: if someone is willing to present something about himself that might make him look less than heroic, perfect, or stellar in your eyes, he is confident enough in himself to share with you, and from sharing you gain a true, honest, emotionally authentic connection to him. Any man can say that you're sexy, and that he wants to have sex with you. But ask him what he did toward the demise of his last relationship and listen to see if he is willing to admit any culpability or if he has any self-awareness about why the relationship failed.

If you ask emotionally open-ended questions and he doesn't answer any or offer anything about himself, he is not looking to become soulfully involved with you. It's that simple. Granted, it can be hard to walk away, but know that in the long run you will feel better about yourself by partnering with someone more like you. And if you say, But what if I give him more time? Maybe he's just not comfortable revealing that about himself yet. Fine. Ask him what he is comfortable talking about. And remember, suspend physical involvement until he is willing to tell you experiences where he begins to reveal actions that have made him anxious, nervous, fearful, or scared. These are the feelings that allow us to grow in our emotional development, and thus their importance in our lives and the *importance* that someone is able to share them with you. If someone cannot share experiences where he has felt these emotions, then this is a sign to go even slower. If he is growing in life, and taking chances and learning from those experiences, he will have stories to share with you that reveal nervousness, anxiousness, fear, hurt. If he is not continuing to grow in his emotional development, he will either not have a story to share with you or he may share a story from childhood (a story so far back in his past that he can disassociate with the sadness he felt at the time). You are looking for someone who is connected to his emotions and adult experiences.

Connected doesn't mean wallowing in sadness or fear. It means connected, able to feel the emotion but also able to discuss it because he has processed the experience and allowed the feeling to move through him. If you are not used to communicating on this kind of emotionally honest and intimate level, it might make you uncomfortable at first to see a man you care about revealing something that hurt him deeply. But stay with the conversation and continue to talk through it because what's on the other side is an incredible new awareness of who the person is and your emotional bond to him for your new knowledge about his life. This is true, honest, emotionally naked intimacy.

Getting physically involved with him too early—before you know if he is willing to emotionally engage with you on such an honest and deep level—is emotional suicide for you if you are seeking a soulful connection.

Everyone has been hurt. Everyone has had disappointments. This is a function of life, of living, of feeling until you can actualize yourself to the highest place of soulfulness where you are able to feel love, care, and grieve without it consuming you. But until someone learns this high level of self-actualization the hurt resides in her marrow, physically residing in her soul, in the mind, in the body. The mind aches, the soul hurts, and she responds by becoming either angry, resentful, sad, lonely, or worse: apathetic, disconnecting from her emotions. This is what I call emotionally stifled development because someone is frozen at an experiential level. This person can never move beyond this until she is aware of this and moves through this hurt to return to a loving, soulful place.

In actuality, emotional maturity runs on a continuum; sitting on the left side, or nascent phase, is the inability to share or discuss anything personal to the more self-aware, self-actualized, emotionally mature place of being able to discuss any experience and its outcome on the far right, and a myriad of positions of willingness to share in between. If you want to know where someone sits on the continuum of emotional maturity, ask him:

What was a painful experience in your life?

What was a traumatic experience?

What was an experience that left you feeling ashamed? Embarrassed? Filled with remorse?

Or what was an experience you have vowed not to duplicate? And why?

If he is unwilling to even acknowledge any experience, he is emotionally stifled.

If he is willing to acknowledge, but not discuss, he is emotionally stifled.

And when he is emotionally stifled he is not able to give and receive love because he cannot move past an experience of hatred or hurt because it consumes him. Think of someone you know going through a divorce and how he feels about his ex. Does he have the perspective of time and understanding?

Has he processed forgiveness of himself and his ex? Has he made peace with his ex, himself, and the experience in general?

Allow yourself and someone else time between relationships to understand, appreciate, and evaluate. Otherwise, you will find yourself in filler relationships, duplicating the same going-nowhere patterns. You can*not* be someone's counselor, or you will be creating a relationship of inequality. Both partners must get themselves to a place of emotional health on their own because they desire to live life, experience life fully, feel a full range of emotion, learn from those experiences, and move on to a state of serenity. From this state of serenity they can each give and receive love. If they have not each made peace with their past, they cannot fully love. It's that simple.

Emotional development varies from person to person. Age is irrelevant. You can be physically young and emotionally old, or physically old and emotionally young, or some combination in between. Think of all the people you know who continue to engage in dysfunctional relationships over and over and over again without taking the time to understand and exhibit the self-discipline to not engage someone they meet just because they are lonely. *Relationships cannot manifest themselves beyond the emotional age of both people.* Therefore, whatever your emotional age, this is what your relationships will reflect.

A very good indication of someone's mental health and ability to love is to ask about past loves.

You are looking for two things in particular:

1. His ability to genuinely engage emotionally, to care, love, trust, and give.
2. His ability to process a relationship that didn't work out and acknowledge his own culpability.

Relationships: Past, Present, and Future

Do you stay in contact with your exes? To what degree? If so, what do you feel is the acceptable physical boundary for exes? What do all your exes have in common with each other? With me?

What bridges have you burned? Did you rebuild them?

How important is the need to be right in a conversation or conflict?

Do you have to have the last word?

Have you ever gotten into a disagreement with your neighbors? Over what? How did you resolve it?

What's the worst harm you've ever caused another—physically, emotionally, and financially?

What have you blamed someone for in your life? Do you still? If not, how did you move past it? Did you verbalize your blame? Was it effective? Did you get satisfaction?

What is your best relationship skill?

What is your worst relationship skill?

When are you likely to say, "I told you so"?

What makes you feel safe in a relationship?

What behavior have you had to apologize for after an argument?

Do you have any words that are totally off limits in an argument? In a conversation?

Do you save mementos after a break-up? For how long and what do you do with them?

Do you believe the adage that it takes half as long as you were together to get over someone?

When you meet someone that you like and are attracted to, do you think:

A. I hope she likes me.

B. I hope I make a positive impression.

C. Here I am, as is. Take it or leave it.

D. I like this person. I wonder if she would inspire me to be the best version of myself, or draw out the worst in me?

What has been your greatest lesson learned about being in a relationship?

Would you end a relationship if your parents disapproved of it?

Do you think a similar background is a necessary ingredient for compatibility?

How do you embrace role reversal in a relationship?

How many people have you dated who mirror the profile of your opposite sex parent?

What kind of partner do your parents and friends see you with? Do you agree?

When does the formality of dating end and the comfort of settling down begin?

What's your favorite part of dating someone new?

What's your least favorite part of getting to know someone?

What do you find alluring in another?

Are you offended if your date offers to pay for dinner? Or are you offended if they don't?

Would you rather be with someone the entire world covets or someone who only appeals to you?

If you were dating someone whom others found not physically attractive would it bother you?

How do you navigate conflict with a lover?

Have you ever lived with a lover? What was your motivation? How long did it last?

Do you believe that living together is a necessary practice run to see if you could be married?

What have you and your former loves fought about most?
   A. Sex
   B. Money

C. Communication

D. Activities

E. Time spent together

F. Time spent apart

G. Politics/social issues

H. Time spent with respective families

I. Infidelity

J. One of you accepting the other completely as is

K. Pace at which you live your life

L. Organization of time, life, home

M. Responsibilities—self versus couple

N. Other (specify)

How do you rise above being vengeful? Resentful? Angry?

How much time do you give to making the relationship work without feeling that you are surrendering your other interests?

How long does it take before you can think about an ex without getting reminiscent?

At what point in a past relationship did you feel that you were too impulsive?

How do you handle an encounter with your ex when you're out with your current partner?

What do you want in a love relationship?

If your friends disapproved after you became involved with someone, how would that affect you? How important is peer approval of partner? What are you willing to sacrifice if you believe you have found your partner but family and friends don't agree?

How do you know when you're in love?

Has there ever been someone for whom it took you an inordinate amount of time for the ghost of her memory to leave? Who was it? Why that person? Did you then look for someone similar? How did that turn out?

Strike the words *I love you* from your vocabulary, and how do you express love in words? With actions?

How do you define boundaries when you are involved with someone so that you're still establishing intimacy and not losing yourself in the process?

If you were married to your soul mate, would you want to be the first one to die? Why?

Has anyone ever sent you flowers or a gift and not signed the card? If so, could you guess who it was from? Were you right?

Have you ever said or been told, "I cherish you" or "I adore you"? What did it mean to you? What priority would you place on love, adoration, and being cherished? Why?

What does emotionally unavailable mean to you? Has anyone ever described you this way?

Have you ever been involved with someone you would describe as emotionally unavailable?

If you were disappointed by something your partner said or did, how would you let her know? Are you more likely to withdraw emotionally? Sexually? Verbally lament? Spend money? Other?

At what stage in the relationship would you invite a partner to meet your family? What significance does introducing a partner to your family hold for you?

When a relationship ended and you were disappointed, how did you deal with it?

Are you content just to date without knowing where the relationship is going or putting it on some kind of timetable?

Do you want me to know you as well as the person who is closest to you does?

Do you return your lover's possessions after a breakup or do you wait for her to call and ask for them?

Would it nauseate you or bring out your compassion to see your lover vomiting because of:
  A. Stomach flu
  B. Hangover
  C. Pregnancy

Do you save souvenirs, cards, and letters from former loves?

What type of person have you never gone out with but would be interested in experiencing?

Have you ever coveted another's spouse? Have you followed through with it?

What words would your exes use to describe you—both the flattering ones and unflattering?

Has anyone of the same sex ever tried to pick you up? Did it make you happy? Did it offend you? Were you flattered by the attention?

Has a married person ever propositioned you or pursued you? How did it make you feel about marriage? About

yourself? Did you encourage it? Did you discourage it?
Did you go along and get involved?

Has someone ever moved like a tidal wave through your
life? How long did it take you to recover?

How do you like to be introduced? This is my (girlfriend,
boyfriend, darling, better half, etc.) or just by name?

Do you introduce your significant other or try to dodge the
scene entirely?

Have you ever reignited a relationship that was broken
off? Do you think of it as normal to break up and
make up?

What is infatuation? Is it a good thing? Is it healthy? Is it
counterproductive?

Do you believe you could love one person in one way and
another in a different way?

Do you know where your exes are now?

Who broke up with whom in your last breakup? Why?

What did you learn from previous relationships?

Which one was the most challenging to recover from?

What's your breakup style?

Have you ever been a rebound love for someone? What happened?

When you know the relationship is on its way out, how do you behave?

What is the first thing you do when you're single and realize your time is your own again?

If Love Potion #9 is your elixir for carnal bliss, what's your potion for moving on and dating again?

After a breakup, how long does it take you to believe there's someone more suitable for you than the last person?

Have you ever recycled a favorite nickname or term of endearment? If so, what was it? Did the new love ever know you had used it before?

Have you recycled a gift, a ring, or some other material possession? Did you admit to it?

Have you ever called your present love by your ex's name? When and what was the reaction?

Have you ever been close to marriage?
What happened?

Have you ever fallen in love with someone *before* you accepted her completely, based on who you wanted her to be, not who she truly was? How did that feel to you? How did that feel to her?

Have you ever fallen in love with someone you accepted completely, not for who you knew she could be, but exactly as she was at that time?

Do you believe in prenuptial agreements? Would you sign one? Would you draft one yourself? What do you have to protect against your partner?

Who's your best opposite sex friend? How did you meet? How long have you been friends?

What do you like most about him or her?

How much of yourself have you shown to this person?

How well can he see beyond what you're showing? Was he able to do that immediately or did it take days? Months? Or years?

How long does it take you to get to know someone well?

Have your friends ever chastised you for ignoring them when you get involved with someone?

What do you do when someone consistently does not respect your boundaries? What boundaries being crossed bother you the most? Emotional? Physical?

What relationships in your life are you most proud of?

Do you keep up with friends and family who are geographically removed? To what degree?

Of your friends, which one possesses a skill you wish you had? What's the skill?

What has to happen for you to trust another with your greatest secrets?

Who knows all your secrets now?

How do you know when you've had enough in a relationship and are ready to call it quits?

Are you stubborn and intractable?

How have you extricated yourself from a relationship?

How have you creatively navigated conflict with someone?

What is something nice that you've done for someone unbeknownst to the beneficiary?

Is it hard for you to forgive transgressions?

Do you wait for an apology? Do you offer one yourself?

Do you remember birthdays?

Would you be offended if a friend forgot your birthday?

Who have you nurtured in the past? Was it frustrating or rewarding?

How many times does someone have to say something before you hear it? Remember?

Which of your friends can make you laugh?

What does the idea of emotional debits and credits mean to you?

Have you ever felt an instantaneous connection to someone who became a lifelong friend?

What was the basis for that sense of being instantly connected?

When do you respond with compassion to someone's ill-coordinated attempts? When do you respond with ire and irritation?

How do you demonstrate your interest in another person?

If I said, "Trust me," would you? If not, what would it take to earn your trust? And keep it?

What could another person ask you about that would make you the most uncomfortable?

Are you ever uncomfortable around people? In what situations? What kind of people?

Are you willing to bend over backwards to help a friend?

What does high maintenance mean to you: an Alfa Romeo or a partner/friend who needs more than you can easily give?

Have you ever been around a person who had qualities that were very appealing and other qualities that disgusted you? What pulled you toward this person? What pushed you away? What did you do?

Do people trust you with their secrets?

Can you keep a secret? For how long?

In a crowd, are you a wallflower or the center of attention?

If you're the wallflower and you date the center of attention, how does that make you feel? Or vice versa?

How have people punished you as an adult? Is it effective?

Is there anyone holding a grudge against you now? What for?

Do you feel comfortable around other people who are genuinely happy if you aren't?

Are you comfortable around crying people? Do you comfort them? How?

How much time do you need with your friends to feel connected?

What's the first adjective your friends would use to describe you?

Do you have gay friends?

Do you have a diverse set of friends of varying ages and ethnicities?

What do you say when you discover someone you care about has lost a loved one?

Have you ever written poetry for someone? What did you write? How was it received?

Has someone ever written poetry for you? How did you respond? Did you save it?

Have you ever inspired a composition? Song? Story? Character? Some other artistic expression in your honor from someone who cared about you? How did you respond?

Do you believe there are levels of love? If so, what is the ultimate? What's the beginning level? Is *in* love different from love?

Do you think that how people treat random strangers in their lives is an indication of how they would treat you?

Do you believe different behavior is reserved for different kinds of people?

What did you most frequently hear from an ex-lover/ friend? You're so ———

A potential business client says he heard something negative about you in town. How do you respond?

When are you most likely to tell someone, "That's none of your business"? Why? When does it become a partner's business?

Do you think of yourself as ambitious? In what ways?

If you were with someone who was as ambitious as you and she had an opportunity to take a better job in another city, how would you decide whose job took priority?

What irks you to no end in a relationship?
    A. Arriving late
    B. Bed left unmade
    C. Bills paid late
    D. Cabinets left open

E. Chewing with your mouth open

F. Clothes long past vogue

G. Clothes on the floor

H. Filler words in conversation

I. Mail piled up

J. Messy dresser

K. Messy house

L. Toothpaste squeezed the wrong way

M. Unexcused belching

N. Unexcused farting

O. Pets running amok

P. Other (specify)

What embarrasses you?

If you bought expensive theater tickets for you and your partner or best friend and told her it was a formal occasion and she arrived wearing something more appropriate for a day of working on the ranch, how would you respond? Would you be embarrassed to be seen together? Bemused? Charmed? Apathetic?

Have you ever met someone who shares the same needs as you? What happened?

Do you consider yourself needy? Have past partners?

Are you laid-back? Would past partners agree?

When you have something to tell your partner and you think she will perceive it as negative, how do you broach the subject? How would you like someone to broach the same kind of subject with you?

What's a situation where a former lover or friend blithely hurt your feelings and you were honest enough to admit it and confront it? What was it about? How'd the conversation go?

Have you ever confessed something to someone only to have it used against you? What was the circumstance? What did you confess?

seven

Spirituality
Questions on faith and humanity

A Spiritual Union

May God help us . . . find our personal best, our partner, inner peace, and a joy to life. I say this both literally and metaphorically. As I have often joked with my girlfriends, seeking a soul mate can feel like a lost cause. But I also don't believe you can seek a soul mate. I think you seek peace, serenity, and your soul mate finds you as the two of you are navigating life toward one another. I believe your daily task is not looking for the next person to date but rather to continue to define your values and live your life according to them, whatever they may be.

At the core of who we are and what we believe are religious and spiritual beliefs. Even if you do not consider yourself religious, your sense of right and wrong and what is humane, loving, and kind is founded on *something*. Look deep enough and you will find a spirituality of some kind. It may be Judeo-Christian ethics, but you're not a practicing Christian. Or some kind of humanitarian spirituality. But I believe as we define who we are and the values that will guide us it is impossible to escape some kind of spirituality, whether you believe in a god, or that Christ is the son of God. You may be Muslim, Buddhist, Jewish, or simply atheist. But something guides you, governs your behavior. And this is what we are examining here. What is the something that guides you? Even if you are atheist, what guides you in determining values? A military code of ethics? And what does that include?

My father, a retired engineer, would say he's atheist and that a military code of ethics binds him to loyalty, integrity, honesty, and so on. My mother would say she is Christian, adhering to the Methodist religion and its tenets.

Your spiritual beliefs affect the development of your relationships in many ways such as your feelings about infidelity, but moreover, the wherewithal to walk away from temptation when presented with it. It's one thing to say you are devoutly religious and to also admit to having betrayed a lover in the past. I'm not passing judgment. I'm just encouraging you to ask questions to understand how emotionally strong someone is under different circumstances. What is an individual's area of temptation? Creative tax preparation? Spending time with a person of the opposite sex but not telling one's partner? Greed? We all have areas that we are vulnerable to. To err is human. To err and do so without conscious choice places someone in a different developmental place. Ask someone what he has learned from his own foibles and see how much he has truly grown from the experience.

Someone who has vowed to uphold a personal spirituality of some kind is more likely to behave consistently with honor, integrity, kindness, compassion, sincerity, honesty, and the other values we define as base tenets for humanitarian behavior. So, aside from having a compatible spiritual philosophy that serves as a mechanism for grounding the two of you, choosing someone who has a spiritual affiliation ensures that you are more likely relating with someone who will behave honorably toward you.

I encourage you to spend a considerable amount of time discussing values around spirituality to discover if you are tolerant of one another, accepting of one another, supportive of one another, or complementary. When a boy friend and I ended our relationship, I was not committed to my own spiritual growth so I couldn't understand his need to have a partner who shared that with him. Four years later, I completely understand it. And while I have not moved any closer to his philosophies, I understand the desire to have a partner who shares my spiritual beliefs and is committed to a spiritual growth as I seek a partner who shares a spiritual philosophy with me.

The Universe Will Provide

If you are single, have dated, and broken up, then you have experienced feelings of sadness, loss, and the question of "Where is my soul mate?" And to this I say: Your soul mate is working his way toward you. And you must believe this in your heart and soul. If you mire yourself in the negative thinking that all men/women are bad, relationships never work, or you can't find someone, you foster an energy throughout you that consumes your forward-thinking direction. This is the message you give yourself. Give up saying how hard it is, or saying negative things about past partners or partners you're considering, and think about your beloved whom you do not feel that way about. Allow it to be easy. Everything can come to you easily. Struggle is an unnecessary choice.

Be loving and accept love. Stop being concerned about love and simply express it. The question-and-answer stage is a part of understanding who you are and who your partner is. From this foundation of compatibility you can elevate your intimacy by spiritually embracing one another. Marriage and oneness are not about questions and answers and fill-in-the-blanks but about unity: physical, emotional, spiritual. This is what it means to truly be soul mates—your souls are connected by a complementary spiritual belief and united by a universal consciousness and universal love that permeates humanity.

My philosophy of asking questions allows you a conduit for contacting your inner knowledge and being authentic with yourself about whether your partner is right for now or right for forever. When you are heart-centered, the love in your life will grow and the love will flow back to you—including your soul mate finding his way to you. A love relationship, or soul mate, is just that: a deep and resonating soul connection because each of you is deeply in touch with yourselves, allowing you to be in touch with the other.

Religion, Spirituality, and Humanity

Are you religious, spiritual, or cultural? What does that mean to you? How do you define those concepts?

Is life linear?

What unites humanity?

What divides humanity?

Are you prejudiced?

Are you negative against any philosophies or people?
Which ones?

Are you unhappy in life? Why?

What is something you're hesitant to reach out to or for?

Can you ask for help?

Who do you ask for help?

What is your breaking point?

What are your principles?

What do you run away from?

What is your vision?

What is your vision of the future?

What do you dream of?

Has there been a situation in which you were challenged
physically? Emotionally? Mentally?

What's going on in the world that tugs at your heart?

What in our world is most in need of someone's attention? Can you give?

What are your very own personal checks and balances?

What is our [our as in a couple, that community, the United States, humanity as a whole?] one greatest failure?

Do you possess the self-restraint/wisdom to avoid the people in your life who cannot give you what you want or value?

Do you have an inner voice that guides you? Do you listen to it?

What is the one question you're afraid to ask?

What is your life mantra?

Do you give as well as you receive? Emotionally? Physically? Financially?

What can you teach me?

What do you hope to learn from me?

What one lesson have you had to learn over, and over, and over?

Do you find perfection in imperfection? What's an example?

What is beauty to you?

How would you describe your attitude toward life the majority of the time?

What is the purpose of your life?

What do you hope to be remembered for?

What do you hope people forget?

Do you envy someone else's life? Whose?

How do you punish yourself?

How do you reward yourself?

What's more important, peace on earth or goodwill toward men?

Do you feel that capitalism has exploited holidays such as Easter or Christmas? In what ways?

Do you believe people are inherently good or bad?

Do you give trust or do people have to earn it with you?

What are you suspicious of?

What has been your most challenging obstacle?

What would you like your epitaph to say?

Who do you think is powerful nationally? Internationally? In your own circle of friends? Why?

Who is the most powerful person you know?

What kind of power do you want?

Have you ever felt like, Now what? If not in life, then where else?

What's your saving grace?

Do you ever gossip?

Has a rumor ever been started about you? What was the rumor? How did you handle it?

What frightens you more?
- A. The thought of never finding someone
- B. The thought of revealing your naked soul to someone

What do you least understand in life?

What frightens you?

Have you or has anyone you loved ever been treated unjustly in life? What was the situation? How did you respond?

What do you carry guilt about? How about remorse?

What do the high road and low road mean to you?

When have you been faced with a decision about which road to take?

Are you proud of the road you've taken?

What is something from your past that you force yourself to remember so you don't repeat it in the future?

What are you willing to forgo to purchase something you want? What's the item you want?

What is the one thing that is absolutely essential in your life for you to feel completely satisfied? Does anything else come close?

What one thing, if lost, would make you feel a supreme loss of self? Does anything else come close?

What have been your most significant life-defining moments?

Are those life-defining moments painful, euphoric, or sublime?

If today were the last day of your life, how would you spend each hour?

Have you ever done a soul healing where a Shaman spiritually metaphysically retrieves the parts of your soul that have been hurt from life experiences and unites them together again so the soul can accept, receive, and give love? Would you?

Have you ever done a past-life regression? Would you?

What have you had to ask forgiveness for? From yourself? From others? From a higher power?

What are you absolutely not willing—for any return, no matter how high—to gamble with?

Do you need proof of God's existence to believe?

What would constitute proof of God's existence?

If you believe in God, have you ever seen proof of his existence in your life?

Do you believe in miracles? Have you witnessed one?

Are coincidences just that and nothing more?

Have you ever had an auspicious encounter? What was it?

Have you ever felt guided by a higher power? Where were you guided?

What action can you not forgive?

What are your addictions?

What are your compulsions?

Was there ever a situation where you needed to be saved from yourself? What was the situation?

How long do you expect to live?

When have you felt most despair in your life? How did you find your way back to your normal mood? And what's normal for you?

What actions against you have you never forgiven?

Have you ever scared yourself by your own actions?

Do you make fun of others?

Are you judgmental?

Do you think as a society we honor one another through sex? Or have we reduced sex to something primitive and meaningless?

What does spiritual union of the bodies mean to you?

If you died tomorrow, what would you regret the most?

What is your dream in life?

What is truth?

What is honesty?

When is it acceptable to lie?

Who are you most likely to lie to? About what?

How will the world be a better place because you were here?

What's the one nonmonetary thing you have the highest hope of obtaining?

Has someone ever inspired you to be a better version of yourself? If so, how did you change? Was it lasting?

What's your concept of God?

What's your relationship with that entity?

If you don't participate in a formal religion, how do you know if you're growing closer to your spiritual center? Growing deeper in your spirituality?

What does spiritual center mean to you? Spiritually bankrupt?

Are you spiritually full? What gives you that sensation? What drains it?

How often do you go to church or other place of worship?

What does that place look like?

What book is your bible in life?

Do you want to be buried or cremated?

Do you believe in a physical heaven and hell?

How does that belief affect your life?

What do you consider a sin?

What sin do you enjoy committing most?

Of the seven deadly sins which one are you most likely to commit? Pride? Envy? Gluttony? Lust? Anger? Greed? Covet? Sloth? Is that sin your vice? Do you ever try to change that quality about yourself?

Of the seven deadly sins, which ones have you struggled with in the past?

Do you believe religion unites or divides humanity? Why?

If you could ask the Dalai Lama or pope one question, what would it be?

If you put the Dalai Lama and Jesus in one room, what do you think each would say about the division of humanity? What else do you think they would talk about?

Do you have a spiritual guru, religious mentor, or sage? Who is it and what has he or she taught you?

Do you believe in karma?

Have you ever felt that your karma was jinxed or that you had jinxed yourself? If so, how'd you break the negative energy?

Do you believe in positive energy? Do you believe people radiate a kind of energy? What do you radiate? Your best friend? Your past loves? Your parents?

Have you ever had an occasion where you thought you were protected by a guardian angel? What was the situation?

Do you believe some can communicate with the other side? How do they do it? Can you?

How do you feel about Catholics absolving sins through the act of confession?

Are you afraid of your own death? Why or why not? What about your parents'? A spouse's? Your child's? A friend's? How do you cope with the idea of death?

Where do you think you will go at death? Heaven? Hell? Other? What does that look like and feel like?

Do you believe our energies are connected? If so, how? If not, what do you believe?

Do you pray? To whom? Why? What do you get from it?

eight

The Signs Align
Is this fate, love, or something in between?

Cultures create words for the things that are significant to their society. The Eskimo language has ninety-five words to describe snow; a featherweight of difference can be the curse of death to an unwarned traveler. Our Eastern compatriots have more than 250 words to express a myriad of emotions, all relating to affections; the affection they feel for their mothers has a different word than the affection felt for sibling, or the affection for best friend—and all of these are different from the word used to describe or declare the eternal love reserved for a spouse.

The English language is rather sparse when it comes to expressing affection. We have like, love, cherish, or adore.

But the question is: What is the universal definition of each—especially love? In the English language we casually throw the word *love* around to describe what we thought of a movie—I loved it—to how much we enjoyed vacationing in Europe—I loved it—to our favorite foods, jeans, and making love. In essence, we have trivialized the word *love* by tossing it about. How many times have you uttered "I love you" only to think maybe a week later or even a few days later, "Well, maybe I don't really love him" or, "Maybe he doesn't really love me." This confusion over the meaning of the word *love* exists because we do not share an absolute definition or value for the word.

And when we do not all share an absolute value of love or, for that matter, other adjectives and verbs such as rich, poor, athletic, smart, kind, or mean—confusion abounds, not only for ourselves but for those we declare emotions to. This is the point of my philosophy: if you spend time asking someone questions about his values, you can begin to understand the context of what those values mean to him. Thus, the relevance of asking someone:

What does love mean to you?

When you love someone, how does your behavior change? What does love include?

What makes someone feel love for another?

In this way you begin to understand what love means to your partner.

Unlike most people, I do not believe love is a feeling that you find yourself at the mercy of feeling. I believe you make a conscious choice to love someone because love is unwavering, unconditional acceptance, and lifetime commitment. Most people would disagree. Many people have no qualms about saying "I love you," knowing full well they intend to keep their options open for someone else who might come along and satisfy them more. So in essence their "I love you" is an I love you of sorts; it's an "I love you till you do something to alienate me or until someone comes along who can satisfy me more than you."

The emotional havoc is that we have no idea if our partners really do love us, or us them, and if they do love us or if we do love them, what that means, what responsibilities go along with loving another. Thus, we have relationships, but they lack trust, the trust of knowing that it's love forever, 'til death do us part, and quitting on the relationship or the person is not an option. And without trust, you do not have the foundation to create an authentic relationship because in the back of your head there's always an escape hatch of "I said I love them, but I could always leave if I don't like this anymore." This is not love. And it's certainly not unconditional love or lifetime acceptance. It's disposable love. And it devalues you, your partner, and the idea of openly loving another.

I argue that couples who said they were in love and then

stopped loving each other never felt love in the first place. Maybe like, maybe lust, but not love. Because love does not quit. I believe love is the total acceptance of how someone is right now, today, as is and without changes. It's a conscious decision to love someone and this includes an unconditional, lifetime commitment, not just for today but forever. No matter what someone does or what life throws at you, love, the decision to love and place another's needs on par with or ahead of your own, endures even when that person is trying your patience, even when you don't understand why they are behaving as they are. Even when you don't feel loving, you have made a choice to act loving. When you say "I love you," it's not an expression of "You're good enough until something better comes along" or "I love you as long as you do what I want." And it's not an expression until you change your mind—or discover something about this person that you find disappointing, intolerable, or incompatible with you.

You may adopt my definition of what love entails, or not. But I encourage you and your partner to discuss what love means to each of you and I encourage you to partner with someone who shares your definition of what love is.

If you share my definition of what love is—that it is in fact unconditional acceptance and a lifetime commitment— use the questions to guide you through enough conversations and experiences together such that you feel you have an understanding of who this person is. In other words, you want to have a really good idea of who he is and what he is about *before* you declare your lifelong affection. In this way, your words have relevance and an absolute definition.

If it's not love then what is it?

"Like" is everything else—even if you like someone a lot. Like may include respect, desire, lust, even adoration, but until you get to absolute acceptance and lifetime, unconditional commitment, I venture to say it's not romantic love for a partner, it's "I like you a lot, but I want to reserve a way out if you displease or disappoint me." Like is, "I'm still getting to know you, your character, and your values."

I realize that I am proposing a radical definition for the word *love*, but I think we have abused the word for so long, we have abused commitment to another, we have abused honor, integrity—the values that honor another. It is time we reframed what the words *romantic love* mean to us and in this way we honor the divine love. Imagine, just for a second, if you could erase the hurt you've felt, the confusion, isolation, loneliness, anger you've felt when someone in your past has said, "I love you," only to then walk out on you. Imagine wiping your soul clean, absent of the residue of those experiences. Because we can, if we elect a new definition for the words *romantic love* as "I am committed to honoring you forever." And imagine how much more meaningful it will sound when you finally hear someone say those words to you and know, that for him, quitting on you, on your relationship, is just not an option ever, no matter what. Call me an idealist. Call me a romantic. Perhaps pragmatic, because I want an absolute definition. But I believe in what can be.

What if you're not seeking a life partner? What if you want a "really, really, hot right now"? Maybe you're not ready for a lifetime partnership. Maybe you just want to date a Mr. or Ms. "Right Now." That's fine. And all the better that you are being honest with yourself about what you have to give—or don't have to give.

This philosophy of asking questions before jumping headlong into a bed full of surprises in an effort to genuinely understanding the context of someone's motivation is a philosophy that works for all circumstances. The questions of compatibility apply whether you're seeking a lifetime partner, a one-night stand, or something in between—including Mr. or Ms. Right Now.

I used to know a man who prided himself on his honesty by saying to women, "This is only sex and it's never going to be anything more." He started out being honest just because he didn't want to get roped in, but he found that telling women honestly that it was only sex had the most dysfunctional result of triggering their need to pursue him all the more. At first he was motivated by honesty and a desire to avoid mayhem but when he found out he could get more sex than he imagined possible, he used the line all the time and soon found himself fending off not one relationship but several because he was sexually involved with several. And somewhere in his translation of being honest, he lost the discipline to walk away from free sex even when he knew that the women were only going to wake up alongside him and try to convince him otherwise. He'd call me and say, "So and so is trying to get me to meet her parents. I told her it was just sex. And so and so wants me to meet her friends and I told her, too, it was just sex." Even if you are honest and direct and state what you have to give or not give, if you elect to get sex just because you can—knowing full well the other person is not in an emotionally healthy place—you are only going to travel a downward spiral with them. Interacting with them is not going to take you to the next mentally healthy place, the next spiritual level, the next pavilion of self-actualization. Engaging with someone who is less self-aware than you is a guaranteed trip backwards. Emerson said the soul doesn't travel in a straight line. This is true. You are only as healthy as the company you keep.

Auspicious Fate

"Oh, but we just have to be meant for each other. Look at the weird . . . unusual . . . random . . . romantic . . . unpredictable . . . incredible . . . way we met. We must be meant to be together. The universe intends for us to be together or we wouldn't have met like this." If you've ever thought this, said this to a friend, or felt this way, then you know the allure of believing in romance and the powerful seduction of auspicious fate—if you allow it to be so. I am not advocating a cynical outlook on life, but an honest outlook. Life itself is romantic by the very nature that we walk, breathe, run, exist. Romantic by its nature of we are here now. And every single interaction you have with a person could be construed as romantic fate directing you toward your soul mate.

I truly believe there are no accidents and no coincidences. The things that happen in life are meant to. You are meant to learn something from each experience, each person. And there is such a strong desire to allow ourselves to surrender to romance. What is romance? I think it is a belief in the positive but more than that, it's a huge relief to believe that some force brought us together. Because if this force exists then we were meant to meet and maybe meant to be together. I believe an energy of the universe exists by comingling lives, people, events. And there have definitely been men I thought I was supposed to be with because the way we met was so romantic. But if you think about it, the way you meet everyone could be romantic simply by the nature of if you are living your life doing what you feel you need to be doing at that point, it will place you on a collision course with particular people, places, and events. This helps validate our feelings that we are doing the right or healthy thing in our life. But it is not romantic to partner with someone who can't give you what you need. It's frustrating and lonely.

Sometimes we hope that we share the same values as our partner. But hope does not make compatibility. Someone is either in the same place in life, able to give you what you need to feel valued and appreciated, or not. While optimism is a healthy sign of positive self-esteem, optimism and hope do not make you compatible.

Time Together: Questions Together

If you did your homework in the other chapters, then you know who you are, you know what you want, you're on your way toward pursuing everything in your life that makes you feel fulfilled, happy, content. Congratulations!

If you're exploring the possibilities of partnering with someone and you've done your homework in regard to trying to understand who he is, whether he is truly happy in life and fulfilled, if he is a person whose morals mirror your own, then you've spent time discussing values honestly.

But this chapter is different. These are questions you ask each other—together. It's the We chapter. Not me. Not you. Not "I want." It's "what can we do together and how do we create a road map for our future together?" In that way, this is an opportunity for a different kind of intimacy—one of physical and emotional closeness because the two of you are talking about a third entity, an entity called We. And that's bigger than a you or me.

Fate, Love, or Something In Between?

Do you believe in fate?

Do you believe in astrology? How do you align astrology with your spiritual beliefs?

What is your horoscope sign? What is your compatible sign? Do you believe in astrological forecasts/predictions/guides?

Do you believe in numerology? How does that align with your spiritual values?

Do you believe we live multiple lives?

Do you believe in parallel universes?

Do you think this is your first time on earth?

If you have lived before, what do you think your life held? And what's the lesson you are here to learn now, and your lesson to teach the world?

What are we doing?

What do we want?

What can we give each other?

Where do we want to be in six months? A year?

How do we get there?

What sacrifices are we prepared to make today to arrive where we'd like to be in the future?

Who will serve as our healthy relationship mentors that we can talk to when we're frustrated, confused?

What's the quality we each possess that is the most challenging for us to accept about the other, but that we are committed to accepting because we love one another and our other needs are being met? How will we manage this quality?

What are we not willing to sacrifice in the now for our future goals; i.e., what needs to continue to be present as we move forward?

If we could paint a picture of our lifestyle together, what would it look, feel, taste like?

Are we afraid? Excited? Or both?

How can we manage our fears and anxiousness?

What can we do for the other to ensure the other feels supported in their endeavors? I.e., in what ways do we validate the other's goals, dreams?

Do we both believe in marriage or cohabitation or commitment to the other?

What do we feel our couple strengths are? How do we capitalize on these?

What do we feel our couple weaknesses are? How do we strengthen our areas of deficiency?

nine

Just for Fun
Quirky Conversation Starters

We each have special interests, passions, hobbies—and personality quirks. My interests include all things art, culture, travel, athleticism, health, fitness, yoga, writing. I desire a partner who will share my interests so that we will be able to connect in those areas that mean the most to each of us. It's difficult to grow together even as you are expanding your base of knowledge, unless both of you are interested and enjoy the same things—or at least are open to learning about whatever turns one or the other of you on outside the bedroom. So if I ask a guy, Do you think Matisse's *Blue Lady* was an ode to Picasso or a ripoff? and he admits to not knowing or not giving a flip about it, then I understand that our spiritual connection will most likely not include art and culture. We will need to find other dimensions to connect on, and those other areas will need to be very significant so that the connection we are not making on art doesn't feel like gaping disconnect. There are some who believe they don't need a partner to share interests, and that is okay, too. You just need to know where you sit on the issue.

Many of my friends are artists, too. Some have partners who are also artists and some are partnered with completely nonartistic people. Of the ones who have an artistic partner, they do have this deep connection, and sometimes that is the *only* thing they share of substance. The decision is yours. You just need to understand that the more areas you share in terms of interests and values, the deeper your connection. A minimum number of values is required simply for base compatibility and a base level of fulfillment. There's always the joy of partnering with someone who has different interests and who has something to teach you and share with you. And as long as you are both interested in the other's intense joys and passions, then you can continue to grow toward one another. If you've ever partnered with someone where day to day you got along fine, were basically compatible, and you desired one another but you felt as if there was something missing, some emotional connection, then reflect on what interests you shared and whether the missing integration had to do with respect and desire to share your passions, your interests, your joys. And again, this doesn't bother everyone. Serve yourself and your own happiness by knowing what you desire and partnering with someone who can give it to you. If I found someone who was terribly messy but a phenomenal artist, I would have a different decision to make: Would the emotional, intellectual, spiritual, and artistic connection override my desire for order in my/ our personal space? What is your hierarchy of needs? You can have it all. But to have it all you need clarification, insight, and self-discipline.

With regard to quirks, there are many questions that reveal how someone goes about life. This is not a coded quiz for identifying obsessive-compulsives or neurotics, or probes that could be construed as threatening. These are more just fun curiosity questions, so enjoy them!

Also included are some general-interest questions to get you started thinking about areas of compatibility. But have fun coming up with your own based on what intrigues you about the world, people, things . . . life in general. Think of these not as a trivia quiz, but more of a, "I wonder what he has been exposed to that I haven't, and I wonder what experiences in life led him to be able to answer these and teach me something new." In other words, these questions give you an opportunity to read between the lines of another's life experiences and help you open doors to more significant value-based areas of compatibility.

General Knowledge/Culture Questions

What state were you born in? What year did that state join the Union? What's the state flower? How about the state bird?

Are there any over-the-counter or prescription medications that you take regularly?

Why do men get sheepish when women discuss yeast infections and periods?

What's your favorite curse word? Why?

When was the last time you lay in the grass and looked up in the sky for shapes in the clouds? What shapes did you see?

Why is the sky blue?

Why do planes stay in the air?

What are ten things you'd like to do before you die?

If you were a film critic, how would you compare and contrast *Crouching Tiger, Hidden Dragon* to *Gone With the Wind?* Or, use any of your favorite movies.

What book stunned you into silence by its brilliance?

What one artist fills you with joy when you admire his/her work?

Do you know the difference between a dessert spoon and a soup spoon? A pie fork and a salad fork?

Can you name a professional athlete?

What's the average score in hockey?

How many words can you rhyme with mate in thirty seconds?

Do you play croquet?

If I said red, what would you think of?

If I said black, what would you think of?

Who's your favorite poet? Why? Can you recite any lines of poetry?

Can you recite anything from memory? Are you a name person? Numbers? Prices? Colors? Conversations? What do you remember with exact detail? What do you forget?

Has there been an instance in your life when you were sentenced with poetic justice for your own actions? How did it happen?

Do you know the difference between a tango, tonga, and a thong?

Can you find the Big Dipper in the night sky? Who taught you how to locate it?

Can you read a compass? Topographical map? Road map?

Are you a "fix-it yourself" or a "call-somebody-to-fix-it" kind of person?

Can you change a tire?

What purpose does the carburetor serve?

What kind of car do you drive?

Do you possess any coffee-table books? On what subjects?

Have you ever run into someone and you weren't sure how you knew him/her? How did you handle it?

Have you ever run into someone and not been able to remember if you were lovers? How'd you handle it?

What's one of your favorite words? Why?

Are you a good speller?

Have you ever won a spelling bee?

Would you be a good lifeline on *Who Wants to Be a Millionaire?*

What subjects are you best at?

What subjects are you the worst at?

What country other than Russia borders Afghanistan?

How many continents are there? Can you name them?

Have you ever seen an opera? Did you fall asleep during the performance? How about the ballet? A children's school play?

What is a shallot?

Have you ever eaten mussels?

How many senators are there in Congress?

How many feet in a mile?

How many ounces in a pound?

How many liters in a gallon?

Where is the Liberty Bell?

What's the highest peak in the world? In the United States?

How much did the Dutch pay the Native Americans for Manhattan Island?

If you could choose just one of the following, which one would you pick:
- A. a personal assistant to manage your Day-Timer and run your errands
- B. couture wardrobe
- C. 50-yard-line box seats at Super Bowl
- D. tickets to Wimbledon
- E. bigger breasts/bigger penis
- F. investment advice from the chairman of the Federal Reserve
- G. the brain of Einstein
- H. Space travel

If you could have a date with a Hollywood icon, whom would you choose?

If you could do anything in the world, what would it be?

Have you ever seen something or someone and thought, Oh wow, I want that, and known that it was completely irrational but you still just absolutely couldn't stop the craving?

If you could work undercover and see how people behave in a situation and how they respond to you, what identity would you take?

What was the thing or person you craved in the last year? Did you get it/him/her?

What's your billable rate?

There's a gift for you under the Christmas tree. What is it?

    A. In-home chef to prepare meals
    B. Car of your dreams
    C. Thinner, more toned body
    D. Wisdom of Socrates
    E. Multiple orgasms
    F. Long life expectancy
    G. Financial independence
    H. Other (specify)

Do you talk fast?

Does it annoy you when you call the East Coast and they talk fast? Or when you call the West Coast and they talk more slowly?

Do you like ice cream? What's your favorite flavor?

Do you gesture when you tell a story?

Do you take Oreos apart to eat them? Do you dunk them in milk?

When you return to a restaurant, do you order something new or get the same thing time and again?

Are you a fast-food junkie?

Do you replace the toilet paper and paper towels in the same way? Is that paper down or paper up?

What's the most organized space in your house? In your life?

Can you walk out of the house in the morning without the bed made?

How long can you go before you . . .

    A. do laundry?

    B. wash dishes?

    C. clean the house?

    D. wash your car?

    E. bathe your pet?

    F. take a shower/bath?

    G. wash your hair?

Have you ever spent the night in the emergency room? For what?

How many stamps does your passport have?

Would you live in another country? Which one?

What states have you visited?

Which ones did you enjoy the most? Which did you least enjoy?

Can you unpack your suitcase in less than an hour?

What must you pack no matter where you are going or for how long?

Can you get ready for a black-tie formal in less than thirty minutes?

Have you spent more time with your therapist or your tax accountant? Who would you rather spend time with?

What one food are you gluttonous over?

Have you ever talked your way out of a ticket?

Have you ever talked your way into something?

What's your bedtime routine?

How long do you lie in bed at night before you fall asleep?

Do you read before turning off the light?

Can you sleep with the lights on?

How dark does the room need to be for you to fall asleep?

How long do you lie in bed in the morning before you get up?

What's your favorite vice?

Can you iron a shirt as well as the cleaners do?

Are you afraid of the dentist? Is the dentist afraid of you?

Do you share the food off your plate?

Will you share the bathroom with another person while you're in there?

Do you let someone share your toothbrush?

How many pairs of shoes do you have?

If someone created a birthday scavenger hunt where you had to drive around town and get clues to locate your present, would you find it charming or annoying?

Which grocery item absolutely throws you into a tizzy when you run out of it?

Do you go to the grocery store for a single item?

Do you make a grocery list when you go to the store? What's always on it?

What's a splurge food?

For what food would you die rather than give it up?

Do you line things up in the fridge? How about your cabinets?

Do you stockpile things in excess like toothpaste, detergent, or cereal, or do you wait to run out?

You go to the grocery store, it's freezing cold outside, and your fruit rolls under the car. Do you retrieve it or blow it off?

Can you read a French menu?

Quick, it's about to rain. You race to the parking lot and realize you've locked your keys in your car. What now?
    A. You solve it yourself
    B. You call someone to help

How do you detox from work?

Do you follow trends or set them?

Do you have a cell phone? Is it a luxury or a necessity? Where do you take it? When do you leave it behind? Do you ever turn it off? Do you use it while driving? Hold it or hands-free? Who's in your cell phone address book?

Do you navigate by map or stop and ask directions?

Do you bend over and pick up trash when you see it?

Do you take/keep pictures of your experiences? Do you frame them? Where do you display them?

If you don't take pictures, how do you record your experiences?

Would you rather have a nice car, a nice house, or new clothes?

What do you do online?
    A. email
    B. bank
    C. grocery shop
    D. pay bills
    E. buy airplane tickets
    F. do research
    G. look for a suitable lover/soul mate
    H. check out porn sites
    I. other (specify)

How many instruments, if any, can you play?

Do you have rhythm?

Can you dance?

Which is your favorite dance?

Did you ever hope to find a partner who could dance with you like Fred Astaire danced with Ginger Rogers?

How do you approach learning something new? Are you hands-on or do you prefer to read about it?

Do you know how to read a blueprint?

Can you operate power equipment?

What's your least favorite household chore?

Can you sew? Do you enjoy it?

Can you cook? Do you enjoy it?

When cooking, do you follow recipes or go with your own instincts?

What does *natural* mean to you?

What foods do you disdain?

Who do you call long distance?

At restaurants, do you tip 20 percent? More or less?

Does your job define your personality? If not, what does?

Do you save articles from magazines and/or newspapers to read at another time?

At what temperature do you keep your house in the summer? How about in the winter?

If someone walked into your house on any given day, unannounced, how would they find it?

How long does it take you to locate something you're looking for?

Do you prefer a head massage, foot massage, or a full-body massage?

What does your ideal day off from work look like?

What has driven you frantic?

Are you a person who feels more comfortable with schedules or are you more spontaneous? Are you like that with all things? Just while on vacation? What about when it comes to eating?

What's the latest you'll eat before sleeping?

Do you have faith in our political and/or justice system?

Do you exercise your right to vote in every national election? What about local elections?

Would you ever have the desire to run for political office?

Have you ever hired a tutor? For what subject? Did you ever master the subject?

What's the first thing you do when you come home from work?

What's the last thing you do before falling asleep?

What's something you do with religious fervor every day? Every week? Every year?

What's a habit you've been able to change? How long did it take you? How did you do it?

Do you have a Day-Timer? Do you prefer a pencil or a pen? Do you have a Palm Pilot?

Can you work with music on?

What TV shows are you/have you been addicted to?

What material possession do you own that you're really proud of?

Would you prefer to drive or be a passenger?

Can you ride as a passenger and not say anything?

Do you navigate directions and correct the person driving? Does this hold true for other life events as well?

Do you ever let someone drive your car?

Do you wear your seat belt? All the time? Do you make passengers wear theirs?

What's your favorite battery-operated power tool?

What does vintage mean to you?

Do you possess anything vintage? Would you like to replace it with something newer?

If you were a professor, in what academic discipline would you excel?

If I were your student, how would you motivate me to do my personal best? What's my first assignment? What can I do for extra credit?

Would you need to be the teacher all the time?

Do you read the newspaper? How often? What are you looking for? Which paper(s) do you read with regularity? Why?

Do you watch the news on TV? Which network(s)?

What's your opinion on the popular sound-bite approach to covering news? Would you rather have the full story?

Do you believe everything you see and hear in the media? If not, where do you turn for the truth?

Do you give Friday the 13th superstitious credence? Do you give anything superstitious credence? What?

How fast can you type?

   Okay, by now you get the idea. Have fun . . . and great illuminating conversations!

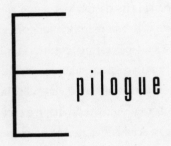

Epilogue

What do I need to make me happy, to feel fulfilled?

Only you can say. This is your life. And your decision. Not your mom's. Or dad's. Or best friend's. And while we can't discount that they know you well, they're also not you. You have to take responsibility for yourself and for your decisions. Only you can decide what you value more. Our parents nurture and guide us toward our values, but as we move into adulthood we have to separate from their value set and decide for ourselves what we need.

Relationships open a Pandora's box for everyone around you to suggest what you need, what's better for you, what's of more value to you. And that pressure can be as powerful when we are adults as when we were adolescents.

I watched a close friend, Stephen, mentally wrestle to identify what mattered most to him after his friends and family contradicted his own inclinations. He longed for a fellow creative partner, someone who shared a dedication and passion about something that rivaled his desire to change the world. He didn't want someone who was merely a supporter. He wanted a compatriot who was also creating revolutions of her own, and he believed that two artists could create music alongside each other without either sacrificing their goals. In fact, he believed that two artists together would inspire each other to unimaginable greatness. And he wanted to be in the company of greatness.

His mother and friends all thought he needed a partner to play a supportive role, someone who wouldn't compete for time, attention, or even the stage. His mother certainly wanted him to be happy, but she was making a decision for her son from her own frame of reference and her own experiences. She had surrendered her career as a world-class concert pianist to support his father, an international violinist who also had grand visions. The choice his parents made worked for them.

It's important to recognize that when friends and family give you advice, they can mean well, and most do, but they are speaking from their own reference points. They can't really imagine being you because they aren't. At the end of the day, it's not they who have to live with your decisions; it's you. Only you know full well the emotional price you pay when you don't follow your dreams, your aspirations, your needs.

This is what makes us real and human: the fact that we can admit *we are only human*. Sometimes it's really nice to come home and crawl into someone's arms and fall asleep, even if you know it's not going to last forever. Sometimes you need something right then. Forgive yourself if you have tripped. Forgive yourself for the tripping you will do in the future. We always get what we ask for. It's a law of the universe. If you don't have what you really want, then consider what you've been asking for.

Is that to say my next relationship is the *one?* Who's to say? What I do know is that I am not angry at the universe for my life. I am not angry at my exes, my parents, or myself. I own my actions. I accept my culpability. And I'm not sad or lonely. I am content. Fulfilled. I am living my dream. I am surrounded by people who care about me, who value me. And I believe that a partner will appear (or not) when he is supposed to and in the meantime, life is grand and I am at peace because I am living the most authentic life. I invite you to share that same space alongside me.

As my closing thoughts to you, I share with you a poem of poignancy, written from my own experiences. The poem "Love's Eternal Fire," is an expression of love as I imagine it for you and for myself, a love so filled with compatibility, euphoria, passion, adventure, intrigue, and fun, that it's as if you and your partner are on fire together. With this, I leave you with your reflections, and hopefully your own hope, optimism, and faith in love as I have described it. May you find the love and joy in life that is divinely intended for all of us.

Love's Eternal Fire

We should all know a love
That sets us afire
And releases us
   from the ordinary
And throws us headlong
   into eternal bliss
The bliss of carnal,
   spiritual, intellectual
Union
Love's pyre
I beg thee
To seize me
Stop teasing me of your
   existence
Winds flutter, your breath
   near mine
Toying, teasing
Glib with nearness
I beg thee
To toss a match
Strike a stone
I beg thee
To set me on fire
Let me know
   the flaming madness

The intense heat
So overwhelming
   I melt at your feet
I beg thee, love
Come to me
And set me on fire
Let burning lust
Be my bedside
   companion
'Til morning dawn
   rises
Love's eternal fire
Burns brightly in
   my soul

—Laurie Seale

Selected Readings

Avoiding Who's Wrong, http:www.licoc.org/sg/whos_right.htm

Baggett, Bart. *The Secrets to Making Love Happen: Mastering Your Relationships Using Handwriting Analysis and NLP*. Dallas, TX: Empresse Publishing, 1993.

Branden, Nathaniel, Ph.D. *The Art of Living Consciously: The Power of Awareness to Transform Everyday Life*. New York: Fireside, 1999.

Branden, Nathaniel, Ph.D. *Six Pillars of Self-Esteem*. New York: Bantam, 1995.

Buscaglia, Leo F. *Love: What Life Is All About*. New York: Ballantine Books, 1996.

Depression & Self Concept, www.indstae.edu/shp/Self%20concept-.htm

Deng Ming-Dao. *Everyday Tao: Living with Balance and Harmony*. San Francisco: HarperSanFrancisco, 1996.

De Angelis, Barbara, Ph.D. *Are You the One for Me? Knowing Who's Right and Avoiding Who's Wrong.* New York: Dell, 1993.

Farhi, Donna. *Bringing Yoga to Life: The Everyday Practice of Enlightened Living.* New York: HarperCollins, 2003.

Fein, Ellen, and Sherrie Schneider. *The Rules: Time-Tested Secrets for Capturing the Heart of Mr. Right.* New York: Warner Books, 1995.

Hamburg, Sam R., Ph.D. *Will Our Love Last? A Couple's Road Map.* New York: Simon & Schuster, 2000.

Hendrix, Harville, Ph.D. *Getting the Love You Want: A Guide for Couples.* New York: Harper & Row, 1998.

Lasater, Judith, Ph.D., P.T. *Living Your Yoga: Finding the Spiritual in Everyday Life.* Berkeley, CA: Rodmell Press, 2000.

McGraw, Phillip C., Ph.D., *The Relationship Rescue Workbook: Exercises and Self-Tests to Help You Reconnect with Your Partner.* New York: Hyperion, 2000.

Olson, David H., and Amy K. Olson. *Empowering Couples: Building on Your Strengths.* Atlanta: Life Innovations, Inc., 2000.

Peck, M. Scott, M.D. *The Road Less Traveled: A New Psychology of Love, Traditional Values and Spiritual Growth.* New York: Simon & Schuster, 1978.

Personality Qualities that contribute to relationship success, www.licoc.org/sg/whos_right.htm

Reiss, Steven, Ph.D. *Who Am I? The 16 Basic Desires That Motivate Our Actions and Define Our Personalities.* New York: Tarcher, 2000.

Ruiz, Don Miguel. *The Mastery of Love.* San Rafael, CA: Amber Allen Publishing, 1999.

Schnarch, David, Ph.D. *Passionate Marriage: Keeping Love and Intimacy Alive in a Committed Relationship.* New York: Henry Holt and Company, Inc., 1997.

Shield, Benjamin. *Handbook for the Heart: Original Writings on Love*. New York: Little, Brown and Company, 1996.

Shoshanna, Brenda, Ph.D. *Why Men Leave*. New York: Berkley Publishing, 1999.

Sills, Judith, Ph.D. *Excess Baggage: Getting Out of Your Own Way*. New York: Penguin, 1993.

———. *Falling in Love for all the Right Reasons: How to Find Your Soul Mate*. New York: Center Street Time Warner Book Group, 2005.

———. *Finding the Love of Your Life: Ten Principles for Choosing the Right Marriage Partner*. Wheaton, IL: Tyndale House Publishers, 1992.

———. *A Fine Romance: The Passage of Courtship from Meeting to Marriage*. New York: Ballantine Books, 1993.

———. *How to Know if Someone Is Worth Pursuing in Two Dates or Less*. Nashville, TN: Thomas Nelson Publishers, 1999.

———. *How to Stop Looking for Someone Perfect and Find Someone to Love*. New York: Ballantine Books, 1984.

———. *Loving Men More, Needing Men Less*. New York: Penguin Books, 1996.

What Is Self Esteem? Parent Education Network, 1 (877) 900-9736, www.parenteducationnetwork.ca

About the Author

Upon completing this book, it earned attention abroad and was first published in Germany. As the content generated more controversy stateside, Laurie was awarded a talk radio host position in Dallas, while also serving as a spokesperson and international columnist for Match.com. From there, she was invited to be the publisher and content director for True.com, another online relationship site. Most recently, she guest starred as a television talk host for the Q Network's weekly segment entitled *Straight Talk on Life and Love*.

Although her advertising career utilized her creative skills and knowledge of behavior, Laurie felt a longing for even more creativity. Thus, in addition to being an author, she also works as a full-time artist, specializing in tactile creations because they trigger the senses. For Laurie, art is an emotional hieroglyphic, a map back to oneself, an experience, a conduit toward understanding and acceptance. Laurie's favorite color is white because it is the color that absorbs all others, and expresses everything.

It is the author's hope that this book defines and sets a course for singles everywhere to discover unconditional love for themselves as well as others. Often people find themselves trapped in patterns, which are the result of subconscious social messaging. In this book, the author illustrates the contradictions between what people say they desire in life, how they attempt to satiate that desire, and how social messaging influences these decisions.

The author lives in Dallas, Texas.

She values your input and welcomes intellectual discourse. Thus, she encourages you to share your story whether you disagree or agree with her philosophy, or if it has served as a catalyst for positive change in your life. A true Renaissance woman, Laurie is involved in many projects including radio and television. For more information on Laurie, her art, her radio/television show, or to contact her:

www.sixfootblonde.net
laurie@sixfootblonde.net

6'blonde^{SM}